THE VIRTUOUS CYBORG

First published in 2018
by Eyewear Publishing Ltd
Suite 38, 19-21 Crawford Street
London, W1H 1PJ
United Kingdom

Graphic design by Edwin Smet
Author photograph by Adria Smiley
Printed in England by TJ International Ltd, Padstow, Cornwall

Set in Bembo 12 / 15 pt
ISBN 978-1-912477-00-5

WWW.EYEWEARPUBLISHING.COM

CHRIS BATEMAN

THE VIRTUOUS CYBORG

 EYEWEAR PUBLISHING

Praise for *The Virtuous Cyborg*

The future is coming at us fast, and Chris Bateman is a masterful guide to the most urgent questions we face there. How will we do good in a future where nearly every action we take is in partnership with a machine, a robot, or an artificial intelligence that shapes, augments and reprograms our own ethics with a code we don't control? Can we tell the difference between the technologies that bring out the best in us, and the ones that bring out the worst? Will we be able to put up a collective resistance if we need to? I can see no better way to immerse yourself in the strange new dilemmas of the future than to read this wonderful, mind-bending book.
Jane McGonigal, Ph.D, author of New York Times *bestsellers* Reality is Broken *and* SuperBetter

The rise of cyber technology has presented humanity with many exciting possibilities, but also a number of pressing problems. We urgently need to examine our relationship with the tools we have created, or we might find ourselves adopting the machine mind-set by which these devices operate. In *The Virtuous Cyborg*, Chris Bateman highlights our often-myopic view of the cyber networks we find ourselves living in, teasing out the underlying ethical issues with compelling clarity. Without straying into apocalyptic predictions of our impending cyber subjugation, Bateman casts a critical but optimistic eye on the important choices we must make in our relationship with the cybernetic tools we have created. It might just be the most important decision humanity has had to make since we first whittled a stick.
Justin Robertson, DJ, artist, and record producer

Online and offline worlds being inextricably connected, can there be any doubt that cybermischief is actively influencing events in the real world? Rather than a facile critique of the vices of cyberspace, Chris Bateman optimistically explores the potential for virtue in both the behaviour of technology and that of its users. Recognizing today's merging of online and offline life, Bateman's proposal of cybervirtue might be a clever way of sneaking a new gentler human spirit into society at large. Cyberspace is as good a place as any to start finding our way back to who we really are, and to who we can be.

Michaël Samyn, Tale of Tales

Bateman brings a fresh and vigorous philosophical voice to explore virtue theory and cyborgs, robots, and AI, including classical and cutting edge ethical debates. Philosophical arguments on every page are leavened with practical insights, including a richly layered comprehension of the business of the gaming (and new media) side of the digital era. Across ontological registers, as relevant to 'real' life and virtual reality, Bateman intercalates virtue ethics with the challenges of technological virtuosity. In addition, Bateman offers an informatively discursive or running list of endnote reference commentary: the notes are as rewarding as the main text in this well-written and thoughtful book.

Babette Babich, Philosophy Professor at Fordham University and the University of Winchester

Praise for Chris Bateman

Imaginary Games

A wonderfully refreshing and inventive look at games of many kinds – fascinating and fun!
Kendall Walton

Highly recommended.
Ernest Adams

The Mythology of Evolution

A book that's badly needed and could be revolutionary... This matters; read it!
Mary Midgley

If you want a thoughtful assessment of where evolution stands as a scientific theory, read this book.
Francisco Ayala

Chaos Ethics

A revelatory reading of both my own and other's work – a genuine philosophy for the 21st century.
Michael Moorcock

An elegant yet passionate defence of ethics... a pleasure to read – and to agree and disagree with.
Joanna Zylinska

Also by the Author

Imaginary Games (Zero Books)
The Mythology of Evolution (Zero Books)
Chaos Ethics (Zero Books)
Wikipedia Knows Nothing (ETC Press)

For Peter Crowther's UglyMUG,
the game that changed my life, and for the virtuous cyborgs
who played together in each and every MUD.

CONTENTS

I. CYBERVIRTUE

Living with Robots

It was in a small arcade on the south coast of the Isle of Wight in the late seventies that I remember having my first encounter with a robot. It was the 1979 Cinematronics classic *Tail Gunner*, a coin-operated videogame that would go on to influence the design of Atari's hugely successful *Star Wars* cabinet a few years later. Perhaps this doesn't seem like a robot to you, since we like to think of robots as mechanical people made of shiny metal, like the droids in *Star Wars*. But the word 'robot' just refers to a machine capable of independent function – and this is a quality we can attribute to steam engines or jukeboxes, just as much as to anything else. Indeed, since the Industrial Revolution (which could equally be termed 'the mechanical robot revolution'), robots have proliferated and found ways to occupy every aspect of our lives. The computer revolution of the last century, which pioneered the silicon chip and the digital robots of today, broadly corresponds to my lifespan: I have grown up with digital robots all around me. The internet was the cybernetic revolution that brought all these robots together in a network, and we were all taken along for the ride.

Tail Gunner wanted me to put a coin in its slot and imagine I was defending a space ship from enemy fighters. When I say it *wanted* this, it might be fairer to say that Cinematronics, who made this robot, wanted that, or perhaps even more accurate to say that the arcade who had purchased this entertainment robot wanted me to put the coin in the slot (many coins, ideally!) and Cinematronics had sold them this specific device with that intention. As this simple example shows, even before the internet there were networks of people and things lurking behind every mechanical and electronic apparatus. There is almost always a financial aspect to robots, because of the way we have organised our contemporary societies. Someone could have purchased a *Tail Gunner* machine and let people play it for free, but they still had to buy it in the first place.

Robots are big business – much bigger today than when I was enraptured with *Tail Gunner*. Some of the biggest companies in the world today, such as Apple, Google, and Microsoft, are manufacturers of robots, of various kinds. Apple has its MacBooks, iPads, and iPhones (upon which much of the content of this book was drafted). Google has a huge variety of devices running its appropriately named Android operating system, not to mention its hugely successful search engine robots (which I used to support the research for this book). Microsoft has the venerable Windows operating system, which supports a vast array of different computers (two of which I used to write and edit this book). Even if you didn't own any robots at all – which is highly unlikely! – the fact that you are reading this book is evidence that you live in a world infused with and organised by the network of robots all around us, since digital machines were involved at every step of the book's production and eventual sale.

Just as *Tail Gunner* wanted me to put a coin in its slot (or, more precisely, the network for which *Tail Gunner* was my point of contact collectively wanted this), so the robot-makers also want your money. They want you to buy their robot hardware, and they want you to buy additional software ('apps', as they are often called) to enhance the robot's capabilities. It's not a problem that companies want to be paid for the work they do; we all expect this. Yet both the hardware and the software that you are uncritically incorporating into your life affects your behaviour in ways you ought to consider more carefully. When Microsoft has Windows 10 update without your permission, it both wastes your time and puts you in an irritable mood, just like when Apple downloads a new operating system onto your smartphone and uses up all your available storage space. When you download a free-to-play game like *Candy Crush Saga* on a smartphone and fail after getting really close to clearing a level, the game asks you for money to keep playing, in what's known as a *micro-transaction*. Most players do not pay, but even to be made to feel *tempted* to do so shows an effect upon your behaviour.

Is the micro-transaction request from a contemporary free-to-play game directly parallel to what *Tail Gunner* was doing to my seven year-old self? The big difference between my desire to put a coin into the coin-op's slot, and the style of free-to-play game that asks for money to allow you to continue past a frustrating point is the relationship between the player and the network the robot originates from. I can characterise the *Tail Gunner* network as saying 'give us a coin and we'll entertain you.' I could characterise the free-to-play game's network as saying 'we were entertaining you until we stopped: give us money, and your frustration will go away and you'll be entertained again'. In the first case, I am paying to be entertained: Cinematronics designed the game to entertain me and others like me. In the latter case, the free-to-play game developer appears to have designed the game to *frustrate* me, and then ask for money to circumvent that frustration. There's a kind of swindle happening here... albeit in a less obviously nefarious form.

Dan Cook, Chief Creative Officer at game developer and publisher Spry Fox, has an acute appreciation for the relationship between the production of games and their business models, and suggests the marketplace is moving away from monetizing frustration in this way. Free-to-play games have become akin to hobbies, and success in this space is now more about retaining players than exploiting them. What's more, it should be taken into account that the company offering the free-to-play game did let me play for free up to the point that the design asks for money, which could be taken as generous. Indeed, as previously mentioned, the vast majority of the players of free-to-play games do not pay anything for their entertainment. Still, the design of the game in such situations ends up radically different from the kinds of games designed for a fixed fee – as indeed happened in the arcades after Atari's *Gauntlet* introduced a kind of 'micro-transaction', where adding coins earned in-game benefits.

Money plays a role in the production of videogames that is neither transparent nor neutral. The way games are designed relates to the way the revenue is generated, and the pressures of the marketplace exert forces in all directions. There is nothing surprising about this, and critiques of money and capitalism are now common enough that they barely warrant discussion. Yet the extent to which we are being buffeted by behavioural forces of this kind – not just in designated spaces like arcades, but in every aspect of our lives today – ought to give us pause.

When a company gives software away for free, there is always something going on behind the scenes that ought to be considered. When you use an app like JustEat, Hungry House, Deliveroo, or UberEats to order takeaway food, the appeal is the immense convenience the free app provides (particularly given most people's general lack of desire to talk to strangers on the telephone). But when the broker for the delivery you're ordering is taking a 10% cut or more from the restaurant for the service they provide, the situation doesn't seem quite the same to the people running the fast-food restaurant. Talking to my local takeaways about their relationship with JustEat, it sounds like they are being shaken down by a non-violent, digital mafia; they're losing money for the customer's convenience, and they do not feel they have any choice but to comply with the company. If they're not listed in an app, they won't get enough customers to stay in business.

The lesson here is that the design of robots, including robot-mediated games, is the design of systems to affect human behaviour. Because the companies that make robots are indeed *companies*, which is to say, are in business to make money, that effect on our behaviour is typically geared towards acquiring money for the company in some way. This is a familiar enough situation in a capitalist society: you pay a carpenter to make wooden furniture, or a musician to entertain you, or you pay a shop to buy a hammer or a guitar. These examples are not that different from paying a software company to provide useful or entertaining tools. However, the difference is that the hammer and guitar are yours to use as you wish after you have bought them: they enhance your autonomy, and are what the philosopher Ivan Illich called *convivial* tools. This term, which I will discuss further in Chapter 5, describes technology that enhances the user's individual competence and control – to take one of the most-cited examples, bicycles rather than cars. Convivial tools make us active, rather than passive users.

A free-to-play game that monetises your frustration is not convivial, but rather manipulative, and perhaps even deceitful. It offers free play, but is constantly asking for money – and may even be designed to *intentionally* frustrate you in order to trick you into making a micro-transaction to circumvent that frustration. I am not saying that free-to-play is an inherently immoral business model – in fact, I am friends with people like Dan who work on games of this kind and who are careful to ensure that their micro-transactions are fair and reasonable. But some kinds of free-to-play games are designed for mildly nefarious manipulations, just as delivery apps are able to force restaurants into giving up a share of their already precarious income by leveraging the customer's desire for convenience. We ought to have some way of talking about software that recognises this manipulation, especially since we can no longer live without robots – they are everywhere.

The simple example of the moral dimension of smartphone games illustrates the complexity of human inter-relationships in the light of the cybernetic explosion of the last century. This is about more than just computers; cybernetics is a field concerned with communication and control systems, including such systems where they occur biologically – and radio is a clear example of a cybernetic system that did not require computers. The term has also given us a striking new word for the kind of beings we are: *cyborgs*, a contraction of 'cybernetic organisms'. Yet as Donna Haraway made clear in 1991, *we were always cyborgs*, and as I have argued elsewhere, ants and beavers were cyborgs before us: ants leave chemical signals that work cybernetically much like human traffic control systems, while the beaver's dam creates lakes that reconfigure their environment, just as our own dams do on a grander scale. All life is cyborg life, it is never biological-versus-inorganic, as all organisms are systems of both kinds, and inorganic matter is part of the field of existence for all organic life.

What is Cybervirtue?

What I mean by 'cybervirtue' is nothing more than the desirable qualities that a cyborg might possess, and what I mean by 'cyborg' is a combination of living being and inanimate thing that acts with a greater range of possibilities than either being or thing can achieve alone. Of particular interest to me at this time is the cyborg each of us forms with a robot such as a laptop, a smartphone, or a desktop computer. If you are reading these words, you are a cyborg in the relevant sense, since you could not have encountered what I am writing here without participating (directly or indirectly) in a network of humans and robots. The qualities of these networks, whether with just a single human and a single robot or with a vast plurality of beings and things, is precisely what is at task when we think about cybervirtues.

Ethics entered an entirely new phase when people like Haraway, Bruno Latour, Graham Harman, and Peter-Paul Verbeek began to look at the relationship between humans and tools from different perspectives. The Enlightenment had taught us that humans were the centre of ethical considerations, and that tools (as mere inanimate objects) were morally neutral, a position that was already coming into doubt in 1954 with the publication of Heidegger's lecture, *The Question Concerning Technology*. According to Heidegger, humans are not free, since we are essentially chained to our technology (whether we recognise this or not), and this circumstance is exacerbated by our insistence on viewing our tools as *neutral*, which is a terrible kind of moral blindness. The tools we choose affect how we think and act; why should we think of them as excluded from morality because they are inanimate? This is the argument driving this book: technology, and especially the robots we are now using constantly, can encourage virtuous behaviour or draw us into behaving badly. We will not be able to address these questions if we think of our tools as exempt from having moral influence.

Since we can call the meritorious habits of humans 'virtues', we can call the exemplary properties of the systems they form with their robots *cybervirtues*. Thus if 'virtues' are the positive qualities of beings, I want to say that any honourable deployment of the free-to-play business model is virtuous on the part of the humans that wrote the software, and thus that they are, in this context, *virtuous* cyborgs (cyborgs being human-robot pairings or amalgamations – a human using a smartphone just as much as a person with a mechanical limb). But the robots in the network that deploys the relevant software are not necessarily *cybervirtuous*, since I take this term to mean that the robots encourage virtue in the humans that work with them, and this is rarely the case. More often, the robot networks we are entangled within are *cyber-debilitating*, which is to say, they bring out moral debilities, such as: disrespecting other humans, accidental collusion in deceit, or encouraging various kinds of addictions that might justify the stronger claim of *vice*.

The word 'virtue' has strong historical associations with religion, but you don't have to follow any such path to recognise virtue and debility in yourself or others around you. When you tell a friend that she's 'a rock', or warn a co-worker that the boss is 'overly critical', you are talking in terms of virtues and debilities. Nothing could be more familiar than ascribing traits like these to the people around us: words that describe the positive and negative qualities of other people, particularly in terms of their habits and tendencies, are already dealing in virtue. Spats among psychologists over the stability of personality traits might make you nervous about talking this way, but if there was truly nothing like this that could be meaningfully claimed about people, most branches of psychology would cease to be viable research disciplines.

When we think about *virtues*, nobody expects everybody to have every possible positive trait, nor to lack all possible negative qualities. This is a substantial advantage over different approaches to ethics – such as Kant's conception of duty, which gave rise to the notion of human rights; or those of the Utilitarianisms that seek to maximise happiness – which have a more all-or-nothing attitude towards judging what is good. These other moral philosophies, many of which are important in their own right and certainly cannot be dismissed out of hand, seem to require superhuman powers if we are to be good in their terms, and that perhaps makes it too easy to excuse ourselves from ethical considerations. Virtues, on the other hand, are qualities that form a set that no-one would expect *everyone* to possess, and this makes it easier to foster virtues in practice, since the moral standard that they set is attainable by everyone, in at least the minimal case of expressing one admirable habit.

Virtue concepts give us all ways of judging human behaviour, but what I'm interested in here is ways of judging *cyborg* behaviour. So if *virtues* are the desirable habits of humans and other beings, *cybervirtues* are the equivalent properties humans possess when they are acting as cyborgs. As I am, now, as I type these words on my laptop; and as you are, now, whether you are using a smartphone, e-reader, or reading a paperback book. The human-book cyborg is not our primary concern, of course, but it is still worth remarking that the technology of reading and writing triggered a massive reconfiguration of the way of life in ancient Greece and China, and indeed everywhere else where it emerged to supplant the oral tradition. According to Plato's account, Socrates was resistant to the new technology of writing and was concerned about what it would do to the Athenians. (Perhaps he may have had a point, given that one of the things the Athenians did after acquiring the technology of writing was make Socrates drink hemlock.)

When we think of virtue, we are thinking about the properties of one being (since we almost always think of a single human as a single being). When we start thinking about cyborgs, though, we're dealing with a multiplicity of beings and things, for example one human, one smartphone and the network of beings and things required to make the smartphone something other than an expensive paperweight. Even if we constrain our focus to a single robot and its human, there are at least two senses in which we can identify positive qualities – between the elements that make up this specific cyborg (e.g. between a smartphone and its human), and between the cyborg and other beings and things.

The way your smartphone or laptop is designed (both in terms of physical hardware and its digitally coded software) governs its moral relationship with you, and this provides the first sense of cybervirtue, which concerns the relationship of any given robot towards its human. These *programmed cybervirtues* are the internal, private sense of the term, internal to any given human-robot pairing. A simple example of a programmed cybervirtue is a desktop recycling bin, which offers the kindness of protecting against the permanent loss of digital material by separating the decision to discard from the decision to make such deletions permanent. We can call this the *cyber-kindness* of the robot in question. Programmed cybervirtues are always qualities of the robot part of a specific cyborg.

On the other hand, *social* cybervirtues concern how

the human-robot cyborg relates to other cyborgs, the external sense of the term. Here it is frequently much easier to demonstrate situations that show a *lack* of virtue. For example, when anonymity in digital public spaces like Twitter encourages appalling behaviour, especially (for some sad reason) towards female cyborgs. Yet the very presence of these machine-invoked moral debilities points to the possibility of cybervirtue in this external, public sense – the design of hardware and software to encourage virtuous social behaviour in the cyborgs that result from the intimate relationship between a robot and its human.

Already, matters have become complicated. Do we really need two different senses of cybervirtue to understand the moral implications of living with robots? Alas, it is somewhat unavoidable, since your laptop is *always* a cyborg – even before you pick it up – in the sense that its existence and operation is completely dependent upon the humans and other robots involved in its manufacture and design. There are always complex cybernetic networks lurking just below the surface of any technological situation. This is a theme that will become more important as the exploration of cybervirtue progresses.

Yet, for us as individuals, there is a radical difference between the encounter with the robot that makes us into a human-robot cyborg, and our behaviour towards others when it is mediated via that robot. We may behave virtuously towards the robot or abusively (I am not proud of my ineffectual keyboard-thumping when Windows misbehaves, for instance), but in the terms I am using here, this is a question of *my* virtue. Conversely, that the Windows operating system acts in particular ways that are all-but-certain to aggravate me is a question of the programmed cybervirtue of robots running the Windows software. Humans and robots working together as cyborgs made those robots, and that is what makes the programmed qualities of robots into cybervirtues, i.e. the moral qualities of cyborgs with regards to themselves.

When I play an online game, however, and act badly towards another cyborg playing that game, this is a question of a wider sense of cybervirtue – more specifically, the *social* cybervirtue of the cyborg I form with the robot networks within which the game is being played. My own moral habits, my virtues and debilities, are part of my behaviour here, of course, and could be considered a kind of personal cybervirtue when I act as a cyborg, although I will tend to talk just of 'virtue' in such cases. Thus, as someone who endeavours to be polite, I tend to be tactful (a virtue) in what I say when I play online. In so much as the qualities that emerge from players engaging with an online game might *encourage* tact, we can call the players-plus-game cyber-tactful in the social sense (a cybervirtue).

Putting this another way, *programmed* cybervirtue describes how we encounter the outcomes of a designed system that was made by other cyborgs, while *social* cybervirtue describes how we behave towards *others* once we have been incorporated into that specific constructed system. In both cases, while our interest is in the moral qualities of the human and the robot coming together as a cyborg, there are always substantially complex (and usually unnoticed) cybernetic networks lurking under the surface. Cybervirtue, in effect, refers to the moral qualities of those networks as they manifest in the encounter with humans. Referring to 'programmed cybervirtue' or 'social cybervirtue' is simply drawing attention to whether we are making a moral judgement about how we experience the encounter (for programmed cybervirtue) or judging how our behaviour impacts upon the experiences of others (for social cybervirtue).

What of autonomous robots? As I have already suggested, the capacity of a robot to take independent action once launched into a designed programme of action somewhat conceals the way these are *also* cyborgs, because they always involve a human element in their constitution and operation. A cyborg *could* be constituted entirely by robots, provided 'organism' is taken metaphorically, as is often the case. But the question of whether there might eventually be robots made by other robots and entailing no assistance, direction, or maintenance by humans draws us away from the problem at hand. If such imagined future robots were *beings* in the relevant sense (that is, if they could imagine themselves in a world within which they possessed a coherent narrative self) they could possess *virtues* – and if they did not or could not, they would not be beings in any important sense.

Yet precisely the argument I am making here is that we do not need the sentient AI beloved of science fiction stories for robots to intrude upon ethics: computers have a significant moral aspect both in terms of how they are designed and how they affect human behaviour. What's more, this is true of *all tools,* for, as Latour, Verbeek, and Isabelle Stengers have all touched upon in various ways, *things possess a moral agency too.* It is not that our tools act without us, but, through modifying our capabilities for action, the things we use reconfigure the moral space we move within. The presence of a gun changes the moral potential of a situation; ultrasound introduces moral complexities to pregnancy that were previously absent; armed drones invite the leaders of nations to think of assassination as a mere expediency. When we allow for the moral agency of things (even as just the modification of moral possibilities) the question of what is a virtue changes into something radically new and different, and that new perspective is what I seek to explore in this book.

Through the concept of cybervirtue, I hope to draw attention both to the meaning of traditional virtues when considered against the backdrop of our vast networks of technology, and also to suggest ways in which the design of our robots' hardware and software *could be made to encourage virtue and cybervirtue*. Currently, this happens only rarely or by accident, but perhaps only because we are unaccustomed to thinking this way and have never thought about the design of computerised systems in terms of moral virtue. Better design does not have to be about utility (a more problematic concept than we think); it could also be about encouraging virtue in humans, and cybervirtue in cybernetic systems. After all, it is up to us to create better cyborgs – either by changing our robots, or by changing ourselves.

Smartphone Zombies

There is perhaps no better emblem for our compulsive engagement with our robots than the 'smartphone zombie', the shuffling cyborg, entranced by some internet distraction, purposefully stroking a touchscreen as they shamble about town. The term gained some popularity after the French news agency AFP used it in 2014 in reference to the number of smartphone-equipped pedestrians in Tokyo's fashionable shopping district of Shibuya. A rise in accidents had been reported, including at least one fatality – a man who accidentally stepped onto a railway crossing as a train arrived. When the Mount Ontake volcano erupted in September of that year, more than fifty bodies that were recovered from the peak were found to have been clutching their smartphones, taking photographs of the lava and ash that killed them. As one journalist reported, they apparently thought it more important to show what was happening to them on social media than to try and escape.

In Hong Kong, the smartphone zombie has acquired a Cantonese nickname: *dai tau juk*, the 'head-down tribe'. The behaviour – and safety consequences – are the same as in Japan, and indeed anywhere in the world that supports high-bandwidth internet connections on a mobile device. The problem here is that hardware manufacturers have a vested interest in producing pocket robots that are engaging to use, and software developers need to sustain the attention of users in order to make ends meet, as the already-discussed free-to-play business model in games clearly highlights. The result is a confluence of distractions that are available *always and everywhere*. Not everyone falls into becoming a smartphone zombie, of course, but who hasn't been momentarily distracted by a text message or other notification? Who manages to keep their smartphone in their pocket when it chimes?

This widespread and familiar situation offers an opportunity to explore the concept of cybervirtue in a specific context. To refrain from acting for good reasons when there is a standing desire to act is to show the virtue of restraint, and in a time of compulsive software and hardware dependency, the question of *cyber-restraint* is an important one. A lack of restraint in the context of our robots means putting the robot in charge and settling for being a mere digital slave. We do not like to admit our debility here, although we will spot it more easily in others. We always think we have a reason for burying our heads in our phones, even to the exclusion of those around us with whom we are supposedly present.

Correspondingly, a robot displays cyber-restraint when its functioning encourages restraint in its human. This cybervirtue is almost exclusively a programmed one; a robot's influence on its human either encourages restraint towards it or otherwise. Almost without fail, however, contemporary robots are designed to do the exact opposite of this: to make their humans pay more attention to them, to return again and again to the habitual activities that have been designed to get and keep attention. This may seem more a matter of content – software – than hardware, yet when an iPhone offers to squeak and plink to get its human's attention, it is certainly not displaying cyber-restraint. This impulsive engagement with our robots warrants the name *cyber-compulsion*, but we could also justifiably call it *cyber-itch*, and it is something that all smartphones do essentially by design.

When cyber-itch pulls our attention into engaging with a robot, and ignoring what is going on around us – whether immediately, or abstractly – we are in a state of *semi-presence*. This divided state will not usually trouble the human, who is often delighted to be distracted from their situation, and this is, as I have said elsewhere, the Age of Distraction. Yet to yield to cyber-compulsion constitutes a debility when this semi-present state draws a human away from their life in an inopportune fashion, for instance, a mother not listening to her son because she is thinking about *Words With Friends*, or a teenager substituting the gratification of Facebook likes for the artful task of cultivating friendships among their local peers.

As the examples of smartphone zombies in Japan highlighted, semi-presence is also extremely dangerous. In the United States, the term 'distracted driving' emerged to draw attention to precisely this risk in the context of vehicles although, to be frank, cars were already our most dangerous tool, and recognising this supplementary risk is to ignore a far bigger problem that will come into clearer focus later. At any given moment during the day, there are more than half a million drivers in the US who are semi-present, and a number close to this are injured every year as a result, not to mention the three thousand humans killed by having been lured into semi-presence by their robot. Similar risks apply anywhere in the world where cars and robots conflict for attention, but the US appears to be worse than the United Kingdom or Europe for this kind of debility.

Software-makers engender cyber-itch because it is the path to money, and in so much as we participate in these commercial practices, we endorse their actions. Yet who among us can do otherwise? We are perpetually drawn into semi-presence and defend our digital slavery with post-hoc justifications as to why it doesn't matter or, even more absurdly, how it is positive and beneficial. We don't want to look our robots in their digital faces... as much as anything, it is that we simply enjoy our relationship with them; so much that it has become hard to give up. Indeed, we do not want to give it up: even the suggestion that we might consider this course of action is likely to be met with excuses as to why it isn't necessary or isn't possible.

Acutely aware of the compulsive relationship I have with my smartphone, I have in recent years been working towards limiting how much time I spend semi-present around my family, and never take my robot out to stroke it when I am out socialising with friends – at least, not without asking for permission first. As someone who tends towards compulsive behaviour at the best of times, I have had to consciously commit to cultivating the virtue of restraint in myself – and, furthermore, to reconfiguring my iPhone for cyber-restraint as best I can. Notifications of all kinds are something I do not tolerate from software, and disable whenever possible. Any apps that issue messages to me without my consent are immediately deleted. The most conducive feature for cyber-restraint in my smartphone is airplane mode, which disconnects it from the internet and any intrusions that may bring – although of course, there is also always the off switch to consider.

Yet we ought to be careful not to blame the internet too much for these troubles. The problem of telephone obedience predates smartphone zombies by several decades, although it is significantly exacerbated by a telephone that stays with us at all times. What's more, when it comes to walking around a city in a state of semi-presence, I used to do this in London in the 1990s with books. Every day I would walk to work, and every day that it wasn't raining I would read a book while doing it. This required a careful balance of peripheral vision and focus, but I managed it without ever walking into another person or, for that matter, a lamppost. I would suggest that the biggest difference between the book and the smartphone in this regard is that the book's role was settled and did not change, unlike the smartphone with its apps. I read my book during my journey, and then put it away. But any time my smartphone ends up in my hand, there's always 'one more thing' that I want to do with it – a behaviour I'm also acutely familiar with from my videogame experiences.

One advantage to exploring technology ethics through virtue is that it provides enough ambiguity to allow for a diversity of judgements. If we think of morality as merely a matter of right or wrong, and especially if we suppose that what is right is settled in advance, we can fail to appreciate the genuine complexities of life that make ethical thought what it is. It is not that virtues are the sole means of thinking about morality, far from it, and I shall have to bring in other ways of thinking about ethics later in the book. But when it comes to the problems of living with robots, starting with ideas about how we might virtuously engage with them provides us a starting point for a discussion that is wholly lost if we treat smartphones and computers as merely neutral tools that enhance our capacities without any other important effects.

I cannot compel you to develop your restraint, and I wouldn't want to. But I do want you to examine the kind of cyborg you have become and consider what kind of cyborg you should wish to be. In suggesting a cybervirtue of restraint, I invite us all to reassess our dependency upon our robots and the partial engagement in our worlds this engenders. After all, what is at stake here is literally our lives, as the smartphone zombies make abundantly clear. If this is not enough for us to consider developing our restraint and our robots' cyber-restraint, we ought to be seriously concerned about our collective judgements concerning the cybernetic networks that we are all now living within.

Cyber-restraint is the first of nine cybervirtues that this book sets out to investigate, along with their corresponding virtues as they relate to our cyborg existence. Through this examination, I am seeking possible answers to the question: 'How do you know if you are a good cyborg?' For the Ancient Greeks, who set the pattern for all philosophical thought in European languages, the ultimate moral question was 'what is the good life?' The purpose of the concept of cybervirtue this first chapter develops is precisely to explore the question 'what is the good life for a cyborg?' Even after examining all nine virtues and cybervirtues, we may still lack a clear answer to this question. However, what should become clear is that this is not a problem that can be solved by merely asking about the utility of robots. What's more, the fact that we do not seem to know how to think about the problem of the cyborg 'good life' is a sign that something has gone seriously awry in our cybernetic world.

II. THE THREE TREASURES

Each of the chapters that follow consider different cybervirtues and how they relate to contemporary life. As well as highlighting the moral aspects of how we live with our robots, I want to try and suggest ways we might address some of the problems this entails.

This chapter considers three cybervirtues inspired by Taoist philosophy – cyber-restraint, which the previous chapter introduced, cyber-respect, and cyber-kindness. Each of these has a corresponding debility – cyber-compulsion, cyber-disdain, and most worryingly of all, cyber-cruelty. To begin with, however, I would like to share a tale from Chinese philosophy that helps to situate our relationship with our tools in a rather different perspective.

Machine Worries

There is a story, said to have been told by the Taoist sage Chuang Tzu (or Zhuangzi), about a Confucian disciple travelling across China who saw an old man preparing his fields for planting seeds. The old man had dug an opening to reach the well, and struggled through it, huffing and puffing, with a pitcher that he then used to water the fields. It struck the traveller that this was an extremely inefficient means of irrigation, and he mentioned to the gardener that there was a machine that could be used for this task, and that it allowed a hundred fields to be watered in a single day, producing outstanding results for very little effort. He suggested to the gardener that he might like to get one of these devices for himself.

The gardener asked the traveller how the machinery worked, and so the Confucian disciple described the design of a *shaduf*, or well sweep, a kind of fulcrum used to lift water in a bucket from the well through the use of a counter-weight. While hearing this, the gardener became flushed and angry, but once the disciple had finished, he calmed down and laughed, saying: 'My teacher has told me that where there are machines there will always be machine worries, and where there are machine worries, there are machine-minds. When you have a machine-mind, you've spoiled the simplicity of it all, and without simplicity, the life of the spirit knows no rest. It's not that I haven't heard of your machine – I would be ashamed to use it!'

This strange tale appears quite absurd to us if we stay within the bounds of conventional thinking about machinery: as merely a neutral means to be applied to ends chosen by humans. Surely the greater efficiency offered by the *shaduf*, which is both simple and efficient at pulling water from a well, must be superior to struggling to enter the well in person to get water? But as the German philosopher Martin Heidegger recognised in the mid-twentieth century, what we call 'technology' is more than just a toolbox from which we can select what to use for each task. On the contrary, there is a mindset that goes with technology – one that makes our relationship to the world around us different as a result. Once we accept this technological perspective, which began to flourish even before the Industrial Revolution, everything around us (Heidegger suggests) is reduced to being a 'standing reserve' – a resource to be harnessed, a means to an end.

Heidegger gives contrasting examples of a peasant working a field (like the gardener in the Taoist tale) and the same land torn up for extracting coal and ore. The earth then becomes nothing but standing reserve, a mineral deposit to be exploited, whereas the farmer had cultivated the fields and kept the soil in order. Even in the 1950s, when Heidegger's lectures on technology were given, agriculture had become a mechanized industry delivering food, as he himself remarks with considerable concern. If the *shaduf* seems like an innocent machine, can we say the same of bulldozers that flatten rainforests to grow palm oil? The gardener's machine worries may seem absurd, yet there is a wisdom here worth appreciating.

For Heidegger, humanity can never be technology's master, and this is in part because we have misunderstood our relationship with it. We tend to see the task of the sciences as pursuing research into new knowledge that can then be turned into technology. For Heidegger, the relationship is, rather, the other way around. The technological thinking, the view that the world is a resource for human exploitation, is the background condition out of which the natural sciences begin to grow in the early seventeenth century. Technology, in other words, is not a set of things to Heidegger but rather a *mythos* — a way of viewing the world, a perspective on everything around us that judges it by its usefulness, that views everything as standing reserve. We have acquired, as the Taoist sage puts it in the story, a machine-mind.

As a game designer, what struck me most about Heidegger's critique of technology is that this perspective is the fundamental design principle of almost all commercial videogames today. The hugely successful indie game *Minecraft* (now owned by Microsoft) presents a procedurally generated world to players who dig underground to acquire ores and rocks, which they use to fashion ever-better tools in order to build ever-bigger structures in the game world. In a gun game, endless supplies of enemies are delivered unto the player as a standing reserve of targets to empty ammunition into. And ever since *Dungeons & Dragons* in the early 1970s, players have been exterminating a standing reserve of monsters to gain experience in order to increase their fictional character's power. I am not suggesting there is anything particularly wrong with playing such games – what I am trying to draw attention to is the way that the machine-mind, the mythos of technology that Heidegger outlines, is so embedded into our way of life that it suffuses our play as much as our work.

Recent scholarship on Heidegger has drawn attention to the influence of Taoist thought upon his philosophy. Indeed, he referred to some of the aphorisms of Chuang Tzu in a lecture in Bremen in 1930, and even began a project of translating the Taoist text attributed to the 'Old Master', Lao Tzu (or Laozi), with an academic colleague, although it was never completed. Yet Heidegger was insistent that it was not an option to merely import Eastern thought into Europe and its colonial descendants, because the change that was required in thinking about technology had to come from *within* the traditions that had led to this way of thinking. He remained hopeful that this change could come about – although it certainly did not happen during his lifetime.

Although my motive in exploring cybervirtue is not expressly to pick up Heidegger's project, he is nonetheless a philosophical ally in what I am attempting here. Indeed, as an example of the irreducible quality of experience that is obscured by the technological mythos expressed in the gardener's 'machine-mind', Heidegger points to the concept of *virtue* as formulated by Aristotle, which hugely influenced Christian Europe up until the Industrial Revolution. As I will draw out in detail later, the loss of virtue as a primary method for moral enquiry involved the onset of different methods of moral thinking that were, unnoticed, beset with 'machine worries', and which involved the reduction of everything to standing reserve that so troubled Heidegger.

As is hopefully already clear, this investigation of cybervirtue entails taking traditional concepts of virtue and considering how they relate to our relationship with our robots and with the other cyborgs we live with. However, as my beginning with a discussion of Taoist thought and Heidegger's philosophy hopefully makes clear, when drawing from virtue traditions, we do not need to be constrained to European or Christian ideas, even though these are the most familiar to us. The virtue perspectives of other cultures, including the Chinese traditions that will be the focus of this chapter, have something unique and significant to offer, particularly in the context of thinking about the ethical implications of technology. I broadly agree with Heidegger that we will not solve our problems by simply grafting Eastern thought onto our European perspective – but I am more optimistic that an encounter with some of the world's oldest virtue ethics traditions (Confucian teaching and Taoist philosophy) has something significant to offer to our understanding of cybervirtue.

In the Taoist traditions, three particular virtues are highlighted by the Old Master as the greatest and most important. Firstly, compassion (or pity), which he claims is a requirement to be truly brave, since if bravery is not motivated by something like this – as in the case of a parent protecting their children – it is merely recklessness. Secondly, frugality (or simplicity), since only by being frugal is it possible to be generous (a wasteful person has nothing left to be charitable with!). Finally, a refusal to be the 'first among all things under heaven', since it is only by being humble in this way that it is possible to become the most honoured of ministers. This latter quality can be seen as a radical concept of equality, since in Taoist thought *all things are equal with respect to the Tao*, meaning humans have no business abusing animals, or indeed each other. This kind of far-reaching humility transcends the more humanist tradition of this virtue in the European traditions, and presumably would extend to robots as well as living beings.

While pity and compassion are qualities that many people today still recognise as virtues, frugality and simplicity receive lip service as desirable traits, at most, and humility (refusal to be foremost) seems to have disappeared in a time of self-aggrandisement and digital vanity. Nonetheless, I set myself the task of working these Taoist virtues into cybervirtues, not as an attempt to embody Taoist virtue, as such – all translation is betrayal, as the Italian saying goes – but rather to explore cybervirtue by taking the Taoist sages as a stepping point. Because I am at best an interloper in Chinese virtue traditions, I will inevitably cross-breed the Old Master's influence with the Enlightenment practices that inform ethical thought in those nations descended from European traditions. These are hybrid virtues for the human-robot cyborgs we have become, and I must apologise for any violence I might be inflicting on the original practices I am hammering into new forms.

The idea of simplicity or frugality strikes a chord with me as the virtue of restraint, that habit of being which is required to attain such a state. In this respect, the discussion of cyber-restraint and smartphone zombies in the preceding chapter already establishes a point of reference within the Three Treasures of the Taoist tradition. Indeed, isn't the tale of the gardener who wished to avoid machinery precisely an illustration of restraint in the face of devices that appear to make life easier? If it seems absurd to us that anyone would reject such a simple labour-saving device as a wooden well-sweep, we might at least recognise that digital slavery to your own smartphone is a failure of simplicity, a clear case of becoming dominated by machine-mind. Indeed, when you compulsively answer a notification, do you not find that you have machine worries?

Respectful Robots

Another of the Old Master's Three Treasures is the refusal to be 'first among all things under heaven', or humility. We perhaps have difficulty even understanding why this is a virtue in the traditional terms that made humility such an important part of Christian Europe for millennia, let alone in China. But as noted previously, the Taoist sage's call here is for a kind of radical equality, and for this reason I shall substitute for humility the related virtue of *respect*, which as descendants of the Enlightenment we are perhaps more open to valuing. To be humble is to avoid placing oneself above others, after all, and thus our veneration of ideals of equality could be seen as a kind of humility, provided we understand how we came to think of humans as equals in the first place.

Although it would be a simplification to suggest that Enlightenment philosophy could be reduced to the work of Immanuel Kant, we will not go far wrong using his philosophy as a guide to this pivotal era of European thought. Put briefly, Kant's unique perspective on moral life was to extend at least a minimum level of respect to *all* humans, even those whom we might judge reprehensible. It is from this philosophy that the contemporary concept of 'inalienable' human rights descends. The ideal of equality between humans was founded, therefore, upon *never* denying a basic level of respect to *anyone*. Despite our continued insistence that we value equality, we are doing worse, year after year, at practicing mutual respect towards our fellow humans.

Displaying respect means treating other cyborgs as equally worthwhile beings. It is not enough to think or say that you respect others: respect is shown by actions (including speech); it is not some subterranean quality to be measured in secret. While it is (in principle) not hard to respect cyborgs that you like, maintaining respect for those you *do not like* is an especial moral challenge everyone of us faces, and few of us master – or even desire to do so. This is what Kant's 'mutual respect' is asking for... but why would we want to respect *all* other people, particularly those who do not treat us with re-spect?

One reason is that virtues are habits, and it is only by practicing something that we secure our habits as skills. This is just as true of moral habits as other kinds of skill: if we don't learn how to behave well, we will almost inevitably behave badly – a situation every parent encounters, and ignores to their peril! Another reason to practice respect towards every-one is that this virtue facilitates other virtues; to possess re-spect for others is to open up to other kinds of honourable behaviour, and in this regard there are strong parallels with Chinese virtues that provide a bedrock for a wider range of moral qualities.

Do not be confused into thinking that the practice of mutual respect would prevent you from being angry at people being mistreated, or that it entails merely a kind of generic politeness. There are times when you are not respecting your friend if you do not chew them out for behaving in a bone-headed manner, and situations where the respectful action is to forcibly confront someone whose behaviour is out of line. You don't *have* to show respect for others, but you can't claim to truly value equality if you don't.

We encounter *cyber-respect* when the cyborg formed by a robot and a human is encouraged to act respectfully (which is rare), while programmed cyber-respect happens when a robot acts with respect towards its human (which is merely uncommon). A key sign of cyber-respect in the social sense of the term, i.e. respect encouraged between cyborgs, is facilitating consent, and thus allowing each to make up their own mind about what they engage with. Software for sending spam, for instance, is a *de facto* case of the exact opposite, since it expressly sets out to circumvent any attempt at consent. I will not claim this is unacceptable behaviour, but it is clearly not virtuous.

Regrettably, the corresponding debility, *cyber-disdain*, is extremely common. Robots frequently display cyber-disdain for their humans by forcing unwanted behaviour upon them. Mandatory downloads of operating systems, for example, are a notable violation of cyber-respect, especially when declining once has no effect upon the continuation of this behaviour (as with Apple's iPhone's remorseless downloading of iOS updates). This should not be confused with situations where the human's expectations are not met, resulting in anger − this is a debility of the human, and an all too common one at that, not a defect of the robot.

Cyber-disdain in the programmed sense occurs solely when the network of cyborgs that crafted the robot curtail the opportunity for consenting to its prescribed actions, as with the example of mandatory, space-eating downloads mentioned earlier, or any other situation where software acts without permission. Sometimes, software displays programmed cyber-disdain when it is trying to be helpful: despite having 'taught' it that I prefer not to capitalise 'internet', my iPhone still insists on replacing it with 'Internet', to my endless frustration, and I have lost count of the number of times that 'i.e.' is 'helpfully' rendered as 'I.e.', because the robot spellchecker is utterly convinced that a lone 'i' must be the personal pronoun.

In the more troubling social sense, cyber-disdain means disrespectful behaviours are encouraged *between* cyborgs. This is so shockingly common that it must now count as a debility of software developers that they have not better defended against this possibility. Even that paragon of purported internet neutrality, the search engine algorithm, dips into cyber-disdain by indiscriminately aggregating content by links. As Carol Cadwalladr has attested, Google will quite happily lead you to any number of hateful, racist articles as answers to questions that are offered *by Google* (through its search suggestions function), simply because its algorithm is blind to what it's doing. Here, the software makers' debility might appear tangential – after all, it's the writers of the hateweb that are abusing the search engine – but significant responsibility still lies with the cybernetic network of programmers and their robots that are facilitating this kind of bizarre and disturbing interaction.

Indeed, our robots all too frequently encourage disdain in their humans – especially when anonymity is provided in digital public spaces, a point that will get considered in greater depth in the next chapter. The masks provided in many online situations invite actions unthinkable in a face-to-face interaction and this goes far beyond mere circumventing of consent, and into outright aggression and abuse. This is perhaps the most serious case of cyber-disdain facing us today, and moves the discussion into the dark territory of cyber-cruelty.

The Unkindness of Strangers

The question of cyber-cruelty takes us to the last of the Old Master's Three Treasures, although it was the first that he chose to mention: pity, or compassion. For this concept, I favour the term *kindness*, since simply feeling pity lacks any active principle, and compassion seems to conflate an emotional state of empathy or sympathy with whatever it might motivate. Kindness shows in actions that provide support for another cyborg, including strangers. Forgiveness, generosity, helpfulness, and peace-making are all acts of kindness, and can be effortlessly manifested in humans that express this virtue. To act with kindness is not the same as acting with respect – you can respect someone and decline to treat them kindly, or you can be kind towards someone you don't actually respect (although this, perhaps, is rarer). Through acts of kindness, we show compassion, and this is separate from allowing for consent and free choice, which are hallmarks of respect.

Asking how we would elicit *cyber-kindness* strikes me as an important question for all of us cyborgs. This cybervirtue manifests in robot-human cyborgs that have been encouraged towards compassionate thinking, and programmatically in robots that offer kindness towards their human. The former is relatively rare, while the latter often backfires – as when robotic 'helpfulness' is nothing of the kind. Perhaps the most familiar kind of cyber-kindness is when a robot asks for confirmation that its human genuinely wants to delete something. As irritating as confirmation boxes might be to some of us, in defending against accidental loss, robots are manifesting this cybervirtue in its programmed sense. Similarly, the recycling bin that appears in the interface for many operating systems is a welcome display of cyber-kindness, protecting against potentially distressing mistakes.

The opposite, cyber-cruelty, is markedly more common and, as with cyber-disdain, is particularly likely when the robot facilitates the anonymity of its human in digital public spaces. Here, the very decision to permit anonymous presence could arguably be judged an act of cyber-cruelty on behalf of the network creating the robots in question. Thus Twitter is a cyber-cruel digital public space, a virtual world where abuse proliferates under the mask of anonymity. Yet even public identities do not appear to avoid this cyber-debility, since Facebook also frequently descends into abusive behaviour. In accidentally distancing presence from human relations, our robots are paradigmatically cyber-cruel.

This, then, reinforces the concerns of cyber-compulsion outlined in the first chapter: our robots lure us into semi-presence, and invite disdain for strangers by cloaking us in anonymity. Once removed from human relations in this way, the temptation to act with cruelty lurks, ever-present in the shadows of our digital public spaces, where we find so little cybervirtue and blame this, dishonestly, on everyone else. Even if it is resisted by many, this dark half-world is one that we made together, and we could replace it with something else if that is what we wanted to do.

The trouble is, the very possibility of improving these arrangements is obscured by the kind of thinking that the farmer in the Taoist story referred to as 'machine-mind'. If we look at social networks as neutral tools, we are apt to blame the unkindness inflicted upon strangers purely on the humans involved. It is indeed a failure of human virtue that forms a part of the essential problem, but differently-designed systems elicit different responses from the cyborgs thus formed. If the systems were programmatically designed for cyber-kindness, would we not encounter less cruelty in the texts exchanged online?

At the core of what drives cyber-cruelty in social networks is *moral horror*, which is another name for what psychologists term 'cognitive dissonance'. When we encounter a perspective that differs from our own fundamental understanding of the way things are (or should be), we experience a jarring confusion that frequently manifests as fury. We are unable to reconcile the rival perspective against our own, and so our minds take steps to alleviate our discomfort, either by adopting the other point of view (which may happen when there is strong social pressure to conform), or – more commonly – by making the people expressing the alien perspective radically different from ourselves, and perhaps even by persecuting them.

Thus, when the cyborgs of social media encounter uncomfortable political, religious, scientific, ethical, or aesthetic perspectives, the moral horror that is invoked creates conditions all too conducive for abusive behaviour. Cyber-cruelty is, therefore, the unwitting encouragement of moral horror, from which it follows that designing social networks for cyber-kindness might begin by addressing those very conditions. Unfortunately, this is a greater problem than it first appears – our robots are staggeringly incapable of understanding the way of being in the world that makes such clashes occur, which makes detecting the faultlines somewhere between difficult and impossible.

In the following chapter, I will look at the way some online games have dealt with their community relationships, and suggest what can be learned here for the design and practice of social networks. For now, it suffices to suggest that such changes of design and policy are *possible*, and there is therefore nothing inherently cyber-cruel about our online interactions with strangers. Cyber-kindness is, at the very least, a possibility, and one worth pursuing.

In the online battlegrounds exacerbated by moral horror, we encounter one of the key problems of contemporary cybernetic networks for communication. We are caught between the immense diversity of perspectives that the internet forces into a persistent and uncomfortable collision. As online cyborgs, we cannot count upon the kindness of strangers, quite unlike most experiences of travelling and meeting new people face-to-face.

There is another side to this confrontation to consider. We now feel able to draw upon a vast array of traditions in forming our identities and ideals, as amply demonstrated by the bastardised accounts of Chinese virtue traditions I have presented here. As a result of a fractured pluralism that Charles Taylor has called 'the Nova effect', there is an ideological fragmentation such that an ever-increasing multiplicity of perspectives becomes available to us. One consequence of this expansion of possible identities is the chaotic and sometimes-cruel encounters that occur within social networks. This *chaos nova*, as it might be called, is neither good nor bad but rather the state of being that we have all been thrown into. It is chaotic because it is often hard to see the common ground beneath the evident diversity – although it is still there, for we are all humans and share a common biological heritage. What's more, we are all modifying our organic qualities through our engagement with common cybernetic networks such as the internet, which have increased in scale at this point in history to an almost unfathomable degree. Right and wrong have become increasingly difficult concepts to apply with any reliability... but even amidst chaos, we might still distinguish the good from its alternatives.

To be good cyborgs means to understand both our technological situation and our moral circumstances. Thus the Three Treasures of the Old Master have been presented here as three cybervirtues, three traits that a good cyborg might express. It ought to be admitted that an authentic Taoist concept of simplicity might well mean rejecting our engagement with robots entirely. This does not seem to be an option we could seriously consider, but we might still find new ways of living with robots by engaging with this tradition's wisdom. As the discussion of restraint, respect, and kindness has hopefully made clear, the merit of thinking about cybervirtue is that it provides a means of contemplating what our robots do to us (and with us) that is directly analogous to the way we *already* think about the behaviour of ourselves and others. Virtue terms are familiar to us, whether or not we have thought about this use of language as having an ethical dimension or not. That familiarity is a significant asset, especially when thinking in *unfamiliar* ways about our relationship with machines.

We become cyborgs by engaging with our robots, which also means participating in a network of relations; with those who make hardware and those who supply software, creating an odd confluence of circumstances. Virtue and design intersect. Recognising these subterranean pressures upon our behaviour helps bring our relationship with technology into far clearer focus. When we interpret the influences of our robots in terms of cybervirtues and debilities, we are able to break out of the misleading habit of dismissing computers and other devices as merely neutral tools; we escape from machine-mind. From this newly animated point of view, the

internet ceases to be yet one more standing reserve to be exploited, and becomes something more complex and curious.
If we still have machine worries, there is now a chance, at
least, of them becoming a call to action, and an opportunity
to discover what being 'a good cyborg' might mean.

III. ROBOT GAMES

*As a game designer, I have been fortunate to experience
quite remarkable communities of players, many of which have inspired
me to think about life in new and unexpected ways. This chapter
considers some of the ways games with a social dimension have dealt
with the problems of cyber-disdain and cyber-cruelty that the previous chapter introduced. It also considers cyber-tact — the problem of
encouraging polite behaviour in our massively connected online world
— and ponders whether cyber-tenacity is something our robots might be
able to help us cultivate.*

Lessons from the MUD

Finding ways to be a good cyborg on social networks is difficult, but these are by no means the only public, digital spaces. As the previous chapter's discussion of respect and kindness hopefully makes clear, the moral circumstance we find
ourselves within is one where our virtue as humans, and
our cybervirtue as cyborgs, is interrelated. This means that
the design of the cybernetic systems we interact with has a
moral influence upon us. Or, perhaps more accurately, that
we are embedded in cybernetic networks, the moral qualities
of which are partly affected by our own virtue and partly by
their design.

As a professional game designer, my motive in working on the creation of play-experiences has always been to
satisfy the play-needs of my eventual players. It has not mattered to me whether the games I am making are ones that I
myself would play: I feel a duty towards those players that
will engage with my games that has compelled me to learn

more about the diverse ways that people play in order to do my job well. However, as highlighted in the previous chapter, contemporary commercial videogames are conditioned by machine-mind and Heidegger's concept of standing reserve. A great deal of the fun in the kinds of single-player games I have worked upon comes from playing at exploitation and power fantasy. Yet the situation is radically different in multiplayer games. There is a social aspect to community play that brings in powerful new dimensions that we can learn from.

As the previous discussion of cyber-disdain and cyber-cruelty has made clear, anonymity and technology mix badly. While in most countries you are required to pass a skills test with cars, our most dangerous tool, and even the United States licenses and records the identity of firearm owners in most states, any fool can appear on Twitter or Facebook with a fictional or falsified identity and act abusively towards the cyborgs they encounter there. However, eliminating anonymity by forcing the use of public identities is a heavy-handed solution that would almost certainly prove insufficient for eliminating the problem, as fellow game designer Brian Green carefully outlined in a discussion inspired by the exploration of cybervirtue on my blog that led to this book.

Brian works professionally on a style of game that is variously called a Massively Multiplayer Online (MMO) game, or a Massively Multiplayer Online Role-Playing Game (MMORPG), the most famous of which is the colossally successful *World of Warcraft*. These are truly social games, unlike what are usually called 'social games', which are a kind of viral free-to-play game commonly found on Facebook with little to no social interaction involved. MMOs, on the other hand, are imaginary worlds where players engage in their fantasy lives together, often co-operatively, sometimes competitively. In fact, Brian worked on the very first game to present this kind of play with three-dimensional graphics, *Meridian 59*, which is arguably the longest-running game of its kind anywhere in the world. If anyone knows what it's like to play games by linking cyborgs together with a central robot, it's Brian.

His arguments against anonymity are multifaceted, but I can summarise (and thus betray) his position by simmering it down to three key points. Firstly, that privacy is something we all value, and enforcing public identities would be to reduce everyone's capacity to maintain private information. Secondly, no-one is set up to act as a guarantor for such a state of affairs, and we ought to be concerned about letting any organisation occupy that role. Thirdly, that enforcing public identities is ineffective at stopping the problems of online abuse, as Facebook clearly indicates. Despite the stated requirement of a public identity, Facebook has more-or-less the same problems of cyber-disdain and cyber-cruelty that Twitter has, suggesting that forcing people to give up anonymity will solve nothing. He argues cogently that these problems can only be solved by changing our norms of behaviour online, and that this will eventually happen in time.

I agree with much that Brian outlines in this respect: we will not solve this problem merely by enforcing a public identity that undermines everyone's privacy. Yet at the same time, I am sceptical that merely waiting for a change in the norms of acceptable behaviour will suffice in dealing with the problems of cyber-disdain and cyber-cruelty. It is notable that, in the worlds of online games, 'griefing' – a kind of playful cyber-cruelty where one player bullies another for their own amusement – has never gone away, no matter how much an individual community establishes its own codes and norms of practice. Yet it seems to me that there are valuable lessons that can be learned from earlier digital public spaces that offered anonymity but had less of a problem with abuse, and coming at these difficulties this way puts a different slant on these kinds of issues.

The MMOs and MMORPGs did not come from nowhere. Their player practices descend directly from the Multi-User Dungeons, or MUDs, which began as spaces for creative adventures, greatly conditioned by the play of the pivotal tabletop role-playing game *Dungeons & Dragons*. The imaginary worlds of the MUDs were entirely made of databases of text, arranged to create the impression of connected rooms and spaces, within which players could move around and encounter one another. Players would join a MUD using network protocols from the early days of the internet, creating an account with a name that would become their identity in the shared space of the game world. Both Brian and I played these games at universities, and the directions of both our lives were substantially changed by this encounter. If I had not played Peter Crowther's UglyMUG, I would have been a particle physicist.

A player coming to a MUD for the first time was likely to have been invited by someone else, and as such was not strictly *alone*. Nonetheless, players typically entered the text world as individuals, and since players would connect at different times they were often (if not always) alone. New players were always unknown to the existing players, so there was always an element of uncertainty about the arrival of someone new. Nonetheless, the community surrounding each MUD, which was typically a few hundred players or so, generally welcomed newcomers, and there was an air of hospitality extended in most MUD communities. Abusive players, then as within the larger digital spaces today, were the minority, and would quickly come into conflict with the more responsible players who would report them to the administrators, typically entitled Wizards.

The Wizard system provided legislative, judicial, and executive power within the MUD. While the first Wizards would be those who set up the software and provided the hardware to run the game, many MUDs used a democratic system to elect additional Wizards, who worked as a collective to maintain order and community. Brian was a Wizard on the MUD he played, although I was merely 'friends with Wizards', and never ran for 'office', so to speak. A Wizard's legislative actions concerned the code of conduct that applied, and thus set the boundaries of acceptable behaviour – such matters were always resolved by the Wizards working together, and generally involved consulting the wider community of players as well. Judicial and executive power was expressed by taking action against troublemakers – in many MUDs, miscreants could be 'toaded', which meant reducing a character to a powerless amphibian. Wizards would hold tribunals in this regard to determine the justice of any such punishment meted out.

In the four MUDs I played, I never encountered any abuse of the Wizard system, for all that there were disagreements between the Wizards over various issues, and for that matter between the players and the Wizards on all manner of policy issues. Most trouble was caused, in my personal experience, by lone disgruntled players. All of these cases were handled by Wizards who either neutralised the troublemaker within the game or encouraged the player to move on to another game. Although I have heard of some instances of 'corrupt Wizards', my own experiences showed the Wizard system to be highly effective at minimising abuse in MUDs.

Brian's perspective is less rose-tinted in this regard, and he suggests that it was a fairly frequent event that a Wizard would let their authority go to their head and become abusive. He also saw entire games collapse when a corrupt Wizard exacted vengeance against those they felt had wronged them. Communities under the Wizard system were far from being a ubiquitous paradise, but it worked well enough that most MUD communities prospered and the numbers of MUDs grew throughout the 1990s.

While on the surface, MUDs were play spaces, in practice the division between game and communication system blurred. This was especially so because MUDs provided the first networked text communication system that didn't require manual delivery, like a telegram. As such, many attracted a community of 'players' using them solely as a chat interface. These were the original chatrooms, since players would typically congregate in a room of the MUD's fictional world to engage in conversation. This occasionally caused tension with other members of the community who were using the game differently, but for the most part it was a fact of life in the MUDs that some people were there solely to chat, and facilities to do so were expanded in the code for MUDs as the nineties progressed.

The MUD was the direct precursor to Facebook and Twitter, which descend from earlier copies of the chatroom concept, such as AOL's offering, which lacked the fictional world but kept the name. Yet abuse in MUDs was comparatively rare, and was rapidly resolved by Wizards whenever it occurred. The Wizards were, as Brian warns, a (mostly) benevolent dictatorship, and this isn't something we should count upon working in general. But as with any case of representatives doing their job well, success depends upon individuals successfully representing a *community*, which is radically different from policing a hodgepodge of strangers. Anonymity may still have fostered abuse in the MUDs, but the systems were in place within these games both to guard against it and to discourage it from happening in the first place. The most effective deterrent against online abuse is community – and the MUDs fostered this far more than the latest digital public spaces.

Thus while a new MUD player might arrive *alone* and *unknown*, they were never *unguarded* – in that they were protected from the abuse of others, and that they were watched for signs of conducting abuse. Conversely, a 'tweep' (as a user of Twitter is colloquially termed) is alone, unknown, and essentially unguarded – and these are the optimal conditions for abuse to fester. Twitter has an abuse reporting system, but it is distant and bureaucratic, with no community to manage the warnings and reporting, and no community-engaged Wizards to act as magistrates.

Here we have three different senses of 'anonymous', all of which contribute to cyber-disdain, and thus a greater risk of cyber-cruelty. To be *alone* in a digital public space is to lack a community, and crucially 'follows' and 'friends' do not necessarily mark the authentic social bonds of a community relationship, but merely an open communication channel. To be *unknown* is to be anonymous in the sense of having a concealed identity – a situation that fosters abuse if it is not offset by community relations. Ultimately, *unguarded* marks an invisibility to the systems of justice within a digital public space – a situation worsened by being unknown, and by being alone.

Thus Facebook's requirement to use conventional identities (to eliminate being unknown) is insufficient to stop abuse. Its users are mostly alone and unguarded, and the size of its membership means that, with respect to random encounters, cyborgs are still effectively unknown to each other. This is the fertile soil in which abusive behaviour online grows: as the cybernetic networks increase in scale, community is unsustainable, since humans can only maintain viable communities at a scale of hundreds, and never at a scale of billions. Two Facebook users, even with public identities, are effectively unknowable to each other – and nothing much can solve this problem short of managing encounters in a way that most would find intolerable. Guarding against problematic behaviour is more tractable when there is a village-scale community to engage, respond, and react – while at planetary-scale even robot-assisted magistrates are rendered impotent by the sheer scope of the network.

Anonymity is the root of online abuse, but the term risks conflating very different kinds of problems. We tend to focus on the mask provided by one particular type of anonymity: *unknown* anonymity, and thus miss the importance of other ways of being anonymous, for which I will use the terms *alone* anonymity and *unguarded* anonymity. My emphasis on being alone may seem misplaced. For instance, in his discussion of the problems of anonymity, Brian suggests that it is those who are in groups who are most likely to transgress, and I agree with this claim, though it may seem to run counter to my suggestion that alone anonymity is a key part of the problem. However, Brian's point concerns 'mob mentality', and a mob is not a community in any relevant sense. Indeed, precisely what makes a mob dangerous is that people are *alone together* when they are a part of it – and this anonymity of the crowd (which also operates fairly innocently in audiences for musicians and so forth) becomes dangerous when the people concerned are also unknown and unguarded, as happens all the time in our digital public spaces.

When Sherry Turkle, Professor of the Social Studies of Science and Technology at MIT, raises concerns about the way we are 'alone, together' online, she is not particularly talking about the mob as such, but her work also emphasises her concern at the undermining of authentic community by the current design features of new communication systems such as social networks. Yet different designs will produce different results. It is notable that blogs, which assign executive power to the blog owner (and thus are close to unguarded) and are ambiguous on the question of being unknown (since it is the blog owner's choice how they identify) still manage to be less of a locus of abuse than the large-scale digital public spaces, since bloggers are never alone. Likewise, forums can afford to tolerate contributions that are alone and unknown, because they are not unguarded, thanks to the presence of moderators – who can work effectively since the scale of the network of contributors is manageable. When a moderator 'knows that such-and-such is a troublemaker', they mean that particular cyborg is not anonymous in the sense of being unguarded. Different ways to foster cyber-respect in online spaces (and thus of minimising cyber-cruelty) hinge upon the different senses of anonymity.

What does not work – indeed, cannot work – is expecting our robots to plug the gap caused by scaling networks beyond our human capacity to form a community. Abuse will remain endemic in our digital public spaces for as long as their cyborg participants can be functionally alone, effectively unknown, and inadequately guarded. If there are solutions to this problem (and it is not entirely clear that there are), the most important lessons to learn are those revealed by the stories of the MUDs, the pioneering digital public spaces, the first cyborg communities of their kind.

Should Your Laptop Say Please?

The preceding discussion brings to light rather substantial questions about what constitutes acceptable behaviour in a world of online connections. One of the problems we have in this regard is that it is harder to be polite under the conditions provided by our digital public spaces. Politeness is not merely an arcane code of conduct, it serves to smooth over the rough edges of human interaction by making requests more tactful, and thus less irritating. Yet as cyborgs we are not good at displaying tact towards one another. This is partly a consequence of the chaos nova, but it is also because we are more likely to be motivated to comment when our hackles are raised, and less likely to speak out when we agree. Sometimes, the easiest way to provoke discussion (or get attention) is to be provocative.

Indeed, until a short while ago, my primary means of fostering conversation online was always to be intentionally belligerent, stirring up disagreements, talking them through with those I coaxed out of silence, and then ending the discussions on a positive and supportive note. This worked well, until the game critic community freaked out in response to my launching one of my 'firestarter' provocations on Twitter. It had worked extremely well with game designers and academics, but the game critics were extremely defensive, having been caught up quite recently in a horrific outbreak of sustained mob-driven cyber-cruelty. I misjudged the situation rather badly. I apologised to those concerned, and also began thinking rather differently about my online discourses.

One of the unexpected side-effects of linking most of the human race together in a cybernetic communication and data retrieval network has been throwing everyone, regardless of background or circumstances, into random – and potentially highly volatile – contact. Because the internet was conceived primarily as an institutional tool for combining computational capacities, i.e. for networking robots and not humans, the collision of people it has facilitated can only be considered unanticipated. We are still far from prepared for the consequences of living in the chaos nova.

When a cyborg understands others and acts considerately towards them they display *tact*. This is a virtue that can mean many different things in many different situations, but the quality underlying them all is an attentiveness to the emotional impact of speech and behaviour. Politeness can be seen as an aspect of tactful behaviour – indeed, it is the *easiest* part of tact to master, since it is so formulaic. But politeness is a fairly narrow virtue, while tact is broad and versatile, having the beneficial quality of helping both those who master it *and* those it is displayed towards. The corresponding debilities are *bluntness*, which marks a disregard for courtesy or an inflexible obsession with truth, and *tactlessness*, which manifests through a failure to correctly anticipate the interests of other cyborgs. Tact need not entail lying; honesty is not an issue here, but rather awareness of the effects of language and action upon others.

The internet has made tact far harder to master. When you deal solely with the people from your local culture you usually appreciate what you can or can't get away with saying without causing offence. In our digital public spaces, however, someone from New York or Paris can collide with someone from rural Georgia or a remote part of Micronesia. This inherent culture clash is concealed by the indirectness of online connections (the vagueness of the digital 'other'), and leads to substantially worse bluntness than happens in face-to-face interactions. The mask of anonymity here, as with kindness and respect, only makes the situation worse.

Tact manifests both in what is said and what remains unspoken or untyped. There is substantial overlap in this regard with respect and cyber-respect, but while respect is probably a requirement for tact, it is possible to respect another cyborg without displaying tact. Furthermore, attempts to enforce tact tend to end in a lack of respect. Thus while providing suitable warnings is a thoughtful expression of tact, it can never be entirely ethical to forcibly demand such warnings mandatorily. To do so is to demand respect by denying respect, a peculiar contemporary moral blindness that comes from practicing the rules-focused ethics of 'rights talk' (making demands of others for your own benefit) in a complete absence of appreciation for the ethical traditions that lead to rights claims – a point that will warrant closer examination in the next chapter.

Robots display programmed *cyber-tact* when they act considerately towards their humans in terms of the triggering of information and do not pursue unwanted displays of media or information. Pop-ups are a classic example of cyber-tactlessness, as are embedded videos that play when accidentally touched while scrolling through text (I have found the BBC News website especially bad for this). Our robots are inherently cyber-blunt (although they needn't be): when was the last time your laptop said 'please' when it wanted to download and install an update? Not that long ago, computers said 'please' when you had to insert a disc into a drive... now, they bully you into updating, whether you want to or not.

Cyber-tact can also, hypothetically, manifest socially, when a robot encourages its human to behave with tact. It is far from clear that this ever happens in practice, and all the problems of maintaining respect against the mask of anonymity apply with tact. The root problem here is that concepts such as politeness, consideration, or toleration require a social imagination, something that beings of various kinds are capable of, but are well beyond the programmatic capabilities of robots. This means any viable form of social cyber-tact must leverage human capabilities in order to work.

Designing robot systems to augment tact presents a significant challenge. Suppose a social network were to attempt to train its humans in tact by adding a policing system, for example that blunt remarks could be flagged by the community as tactless. The net result of this would rapidly devolve into carnage, since humans in digital public spaces will always abuse systems that are capable of causing harm. Of course, not everyone does so – but it only takes a small proportion of people to make a minor design flaw into a disaster.

A classic example occurred in the design of *The Sims Online* game. In an early version of this, players could declare other players 'trustworthy' or 'untrustworthy'. However, a group of players calling themselves the 'Sims Mafia' realised they could use this feature to shake down new players – threatening to blackball them as 'untrustworthy' if they didn't give them all their in-game money. The design of 'public karma' systems (as they are known) has avoided dealing with negative scores for precisely this reason, not to mention that humans will abandon their tainted accounts if necessary, in what has been called 'karma bankruptcy'.

Now it may seem that this is irrelevant to the question of cyber-tact: couldn't you just have the robot provide a positive tact score? Yes, this would be the minimal case for cyber-tact. A positive tact system records when people report that others have been tactful, but necessarily such humans must be *already* capable of tact. The robot has displayed cyber-virtue, but merely through tracking human virtue and thus encouraging the use of tact that a human already possessed. But precisely our problem is that the kind of tact we now need exceeds our prior experience. What is most needed in terms of cyber-tact is a way for a robot to teach its human how to act tactfully in the cultural collision of the internet. It is far from clear if this design question is actually soluble, although we will return to this problem later to consider it from a different perspective.

Whereas designing for social cyber-respect may be a matter of adapting to the problems of online anonymity, social cyber-tact seems to be more challenging. In both cases, however, the design of robots can at least aim at programmed cybervirtue, by (for example) affording their humans adequate control over what they see or read, defending against unwanted displays of media, and supplicating when requesting an inconvenience (instead of demanding, as is far more common). If we think of our robots as 'neutral tools', the idea that virtue could be applied to their function is lost on us. Yet we do not use a computer like a hammer (unless we are especially irate!) and we are entitled to expect it to say 'please' when it wants to do something that we do not.

Tenacity and the Domination of Things
Since I have mostly dwelt upon the negative aspects of our relationships with our robots, it is perhaps time to acknowledge that being part of a human-robot cyborg pairing also

has its benefits. There is a distinct possibility that as cyborgs we might show greater *tenacity*. Our robots never tire, after all, and always pursue what we have instructed them to do if nothing disrupts them along the way. That presents an opportunity. Perhaps their diligence can be made to work on us, to bring out our perseverance where we most need it? However, for this benefit to become clear, we first have to become aware of the corresponding risks that come from sharing our agency with our robots. We must be able to clearly distinguish cyber-tenacity from the domination of things, and that requires a clear understanding of what it means to will something.

In the first chapter, I touched upon the way that things possess their own moral agency – they modify the options available to us, which in turn has a moral impact upon our behaviour. But if things have an agency to them, we have to be able to discriminate between those situations where we are pushing forward the chosen actions and those where things are influencing us, usually without our noticing. This was also part of what the Taoist sage was hinting at with the concepts of 'machine worries' and 'machine-mind': it is not enough to accept that a device can make a task apparently easier. There are other effects on our thought and experience that need to be taken into consideration.

Once the agency of things is taken into consideration, the question of when persistence and determination constitutes a virtue will entail some careful consideration of just *what* we are persisting in doing. Clearly, not all activities are equal in this regard. A heroin addict's perseverance in their habit, and their dedication to acquiring money for it, do not count as any kind of virtuous quality. The shift in our understanding of agency brought about by re-assessing the role of things in our decisions gives us a way of appreciating why: it's the *heroin* that is in charge of that chain of events, and the human is reduced to its servant. Much the same has been implied by Bruno Latour when he talks of the relationships between cigarettes and smokers: the cigarette can hardly smoke itself, but the smoker cannot exactly say they are in control of their actions either. Here, as in many situations, agency can be distributed between beings and things, as long as it is understood that without at least one being (or robot), nothing much is going to happen at all.

To construct a virtuous understanding of *tenacity,* we need a viable understanding of what Enlightenment philosophers called 'will' – the resolve to take a certain path, to commit to an uncertain future, and to make it happen. This is distinct from 'impulse' – I can hanker impulsively for a sandwich but I cannot *will* one, although I could will that I mastered the art of sandwich-making, or bread-baking, or that I would open a sandwich shop. But what does this distinction consist of? Is it a difference of kind, or merely one of degree?

The one surviving place in our language where the concept of *will* survives is in talk of 'willpower' – but our current understanding of biology renders this concept suspect. If there were a viable concept of willpower, it would distinguish between two kinds of people: ones that had it, and thus would show tenacity in all things, and those who lacked it and would thus be condemned to perpetual indolence interspersed with sporadic, unthought-through impulses. But this isn't what happens in life. Although we do see differences in persistence, both in terms of people and in terms of activities, a person who persists in all tasks does not seem 'high in willpower' so much as obsessive-compulsive, unable to stop themselves from attending to whatever happens to be in their attention. Both willpower, and the Enlightenment concept of will it descends from, presume our capacity to assert agency in a selective fashion, such that we always appear to be in charge of our own actions.

Biologically, the trait of persistence is found as *habit*. Take the simple instance of getting up in the morning. I recall a time in my life when I had been staying up late most nights (carousing or playing games). At some point, I resolved to get my sleeping back in order – but was dismayed to discover that setting my alarm early made little difference to my routines. Barely awake, I would snooze or switch off any alarm before my half-conscious mind knew what was going on. Today, I get up at the same time every day, and getting up is comparatively easy to do, even at 5:30 am, a time I had previously associated with calling it a night. This transformation has nothing to do with willpower but everything to do with habit. It was not enough to commit while awake to something that would happen before I was fully conscious: I had to establish the habit. This, as it happens, is far easier when we act in the context of other people: exercise groups and dieting clubs establish successful habits more easily than people trying to lose weight on their own, for all that some people are able to motivate themselves independently.

Here, then, is a way of tracing a boundary between will and impulse, tenacity and capriciousness. To *will* something entails founding, then sustaining, habits that are steps towards what is imagined. Our impulses, on the other hand, strike us on a moment-to-moment basis – and when these impulses become habits, as with heroin, these habits have the circumstantial effect of sacrificing what we might otherwise will; we are enslaved to the will of other beings (such as those selling heroin), or to the inclinations brought on by things (such as the heroin itself). While there are certainly debilities corresponding to an absence of diligence and determination (apathy, for instance) perhaps the more interesting contrast is this one between tenacity of the will, and submissiveness to impulse.

When it comes to thinking about *cyber-tenacity*, it may initially seem that we have a context where our robots might indeed foster enthusiasm and perseverance in their humans. We only have to look at videogames for endless examples of cyborgs persisting against rage, confusion, or boredom, or indeed establishing ostensibly positive habits such as physical exercise, which, for example, *Pokémon Go* makes essential to its play (for all that it also trades on the player's compulsions through the free-to-play business model). If we are comparing tenacity to apathy, our robot-mediated games clearly come up trumps – if there is indeed a form of cyber-apathy, I have yet to see it, unless the paralysis of excessive choice counts. Every commercially successful game encourages its players to come back for more, and cyber-tenacity is thus a design goal for many such projects.

But then, whose will is being served here? If the player is truly imagining a future and pursuing it, we might very well call the desire to keep playing a game the cyber-tenacity of the human-robot pairing. Yet when a videogame has us in its grip we are *submissive* to it: our desire to keep playing is often *more like* the heroin addict's habit than the will to become a master baker. In particular, if we look at what the lazier exponents of what is called 'gamification' have recommended, this seems indistinguishable from the Behaviourist's schedules of rein-forcement – habit formation through repetition and reward... dog training for humans. This is submission, not tenacity.

As I have argued elsewhere, 'gamification' is all too often 'stultification'. This is a term Jacques Rancière introduces in the context of education, but it is one that I find extremely pertinent to game design, since, as fellow game designer Raph Koster is apt to point out, learning is a key part of the play of any game. Rancière suggests that any attempt at education is counter-productive when teachers attempt to force upon students *their* understanding of a particular topic or skill, rather than encouraging the student to acquire their own competences. He calls it *stultifying* when an educator teaches a specific method of understanding rather than encouraging learning without specifying a specific form of comprehension. Learning avoids this when the teacher's will is bound to the student's solely in terms of committing to the learning being achieved; whenever the *means* that learning will proceed eclipses this binding of a common will, the outcome is stultification, and learning is hindered or entirely stifled.

Gamification risks stultification because the game developer (or behavioural engineer) is specifying what is being learned, and there is no engagement of the will of the player (or employee). Submission is the inevitable outcome of this failure to create a common vision. What's more, through mandatory achievements and scoring systems like Xbox's Gamerscore we have witnessed *the gamification of games...* an emphasis on what might be called *cyber-submission* over the more engaging alternative ways of offering play. This state of affairs is now endemic in software design: what are Twitter and Facebook's 'follow' counters if not an invitation to judge quantity over quality? Everywhere game-like scoring systems occur, there is a degradation of our judgement, as we are drawn away from even asking ourselves what we will, and into submission to the designed system and its values.

Yet this *cyber-domination* of videogames over their humans is by no means the whole story. Our robot-mediated games also demonstrate cyber-tenacity in the way humans form teams and co-operate towards goals together, and although competitive play often brings out the worst in people, there are virtuous communities of players in a great many situations where their will is being exercised virtuously, albeit within the limited context of the games in question. The player who commits to the pursuit of a digital sporting victory is not, perhaps, the paragon of tenacity – but they are not so far removed from the physical athlete, whose determination we justly admire. Add to this the exercise of imagination in the narrative play of MMOs and elsewhere, or the creative projects realised in *Minecraft*, and the situation does not seem so resolutely submissive.

These examples occur in the context of play, which is always a negotiable, transient experience. But they point to ways that our robots can elicit cyber-tenacity in cyborgs, a theme that also appears in the work of Jane McGonigal. There are possibilities here worthy of exploration, but they must avoid the stultifying risks of cyber-domination and empower us to set our own wills in motion and see matters through. Here is somewhere that our robots have a natural advantage, for they are automatically cyber-tenacious in the programmed sense – they do not tire or flag, and keep progressing towards what we have willed unless prevented by inability or malfunction. If we can couple that indomitable spirit with our own wills without being dragged down into submission along the way, there might be no limit to what we cyborgs might achieve.

Examining the cybervirtue of videogames adds to our understanding of what it might mean to be a good cyborg. When the social networks were explored in terms of respect and kindness, we found a troubling prevalence of cyber-disdain and cyber-cruelty. Yet the MUDs reveal how a virtuous community can be bound together by their mutual engagement in the fictional world of a game. Similarly, online game designers have had to wrestle with the issues of cyber-tact, and through the design of public karma systems they have, to some extent, been able to encourage kindness programmatically. Finally, while there is always a risk of falling into cyber-submission when we play a videogame, there are also tremendous opportunities for cyborgs to express cyber-tenacity through virtuous competition, or acts of creative imagination. In all these cases, what has underpinned the expression of virtue in videogames is a community of players. The virtuous cyborg is never alone when they play, but is always finding the good in their positive engagement with other players.

IV. SHALLOW-SIGHTED CYBORGS

As earlier chapters have stressed, we are embedded within cybernetic networks that affect our behaviour, and one way of understanding cybervirtue is precisely as the moral qualities of these networks as they intersect with us. With the previously-discussed cybervirtues of restraint, respect, kindness, tact, and tenacity, cybervirtue emerged from the intersection of our own virtue and the design of the robots we use to access the internet. In this chapter I want to consider a virtue that is endangered by our current cybernetic circumstances: being deep-sighted. *This requires a diversion in order to consider the technological mindset that so concerned Heidegger, and the rival ethical systems that supplanted virtue as the basis of moral judgement.*

Tip of the Cyberg

Examining our situation in terms of cybervirtue means to foreground everything that had previously been unseen and unnoticed in our relationship with technology. As a starting point, it is important to notice the tremendous faith we have in our machines and technical prowess. The astonishing advances in technological power in the prior century give an impression of infinite capabilities – the closest that secular thought ever gets to imagining omnipotence. Thus we have no difficulty envisioning (if we suspend critical judgment) techno-immortality, sentient robots, or interstellar travel. Indeed, science fiction is replete with these imaginary grails. This way of thinking about our tools – as personal enhancement – radically misleads us in several important ways, but perhaps the most striking is the sense that while equipped with any technology

73

we act autonomously. This is always a subtle deception.

Science fiction helps bring this confusion into focus. In *Star Trek*, the communicator, universal translator, phaser, transporter, and tricorder all do one thing perfectly (except when drama requires otherwise), to the extent that a Starfleet officer equipped with these things can appear anywhere, talk to anyone, scan anything to know what it is and what condition it is in, and – when push comes to shove – stun or kill on demand. All these capabilities occur literally at the push of a button. Where do these miracle tools come from? How do they work? It doesn't matter; it's high technology (hi-tech) – which is strikingly parallel to the magic-laden worlds of high fantasy. Arthur C. Clarke's adage that any sufficiently advanced technology is indistinguishable from magic should raise more questions than it usually does... even in the context of sword and sorcery, we are entitled to ask: where does the magic come from? What is expended when it is used? What are the unseen limitations to its usage?

In the *Terminator* movie franchise, mankind has been driven to the brink of extinction by robotic killing machines, made by humans who did not consider the consequences of the technology they were creating. That much is not hard to believe, particularly when you see the effortlessness with which the armed drone made battlefield honour obsolete. Yet against the backdrop of a civilisation in total collapse and killer robots prowling everywhere, the Resistance movement depicted by *Terminator: Salvation* somehow maintains safe houses, feeds the survivors, even operates fighter planes. The aeroplane sits in our mind like the tricorder and communicator – autonomous once paired with a human. But as Bruno Latour never tires of reminding us: airplanes do not fly, it is *airlines* that fly. In stark contradistinction with what we see in a *Terminator* movie, no plane takes to the air without their logistical supply chains bringing fuel, their air traffic control networks managing flight paths, their support personnel performing essential maintenance.

Technology is not magic, and even fictional portrayals of magic are not as autonomous as we imagine our tools make us. There is a stark difference between hammers, binoculars, and a wind-up lantern on the one hand and computers, cars, and airplanes on the other. While both sets of examples are manufactured by complex meshes of people and things, the latter list also require a complex network *just to operate*, a point brought into clear focus by the actor-network theory developed by Michel Callon and Bruno Latour. This began as an alternative to conventional social theory, one that sought to break down the distinction between society and nature that had emerged from the philosophy of Descartes, Kant, and their successors.

As the name suggests, actor-network theory is about networks of things that act, and one of the keys to this approach is that it does not significantly distinguish between human and non-human actors. Computers, buildings, organisations all have to be integrated into the same network in an ANT approach, and are treated as having a share of the agency being exercised. The purpose is to gain detailed descriptions about the concrete mechanisms that work to maintain these networks, while impartially assessing the ways the networks act and the role of beings and things in the actions taken. In other words, ANT is about understanding humans, robots, and various other things as nodes within a network that facilitates all kinds of actions that would be impossible without that network.

What's more, ANT doesn't treat anything as having a reality outside of being enacted within their networks. Thus for ANT there is no 'society' as such, although there are networks that bring humans into a common relationship – but always with a vast array of non-human actors coming along for the ride. Indeed, one of the principal changes in perspective that ANT asks for is for greater care about what we notice and how we collect things together. A nation, for instance, is a phantasm until we recognise the vast set of bureaucratic procedures, computers, roads, vehicles, logistical processes and so forth that are all out of sight and out of mind when we think of countries as merely lines on a map. This method, and others like it, invite a radical change to our understanding of how we relate to technology.

If a cyborg is what occurs when an organism is cybernetically enhanced by a tool like a hammer, we can call the network that produces and maintains the more complicated cyborgs like cars-and-their-drivers or computers-and-their-users, a *cyberg*. An iceberg famously has just 10% of its mass above the waterline, and thus only its top is visible to the casual observer. So it is with the cyberg – the cybernetic network required by the more convoluted of our technologies. We see only the cyborg – the car and its driver – and not the cyberg that makes it possible. The cyberg itself is nothing more than the cybernetic network of a given technology, the actor-network relating to that particular tool in ANT terms. But bringing cybergs into focus is as difficult as seeing the submerged mass of the iceberg while floating upon the surface of the sea.

When it comes to technology we are perpetually *shallow-sighted* (a rather peculiar debility): we see only the 'surface' of the network, so flat that it can be expressed as a one-dimensional array or list (car, driver, fuel, road). If we manage somehow to become more deep-sighted, we can recognise the relations and dependencies that give the cyberg its net-work-qualities (ore mines, smelting mills, factories, oil rigs, refineries and far more besides). These dependencies rapidly become tangential and obscure: an oil rig has scuba divers who repair the metal structure when it corrodes with arc welders entirely unique to their profession, but who is deep-sighted enough to think of the factories making hyperbaric welding kits or compressed air-tank regulators, when looking at a car?

It is the cyberg that defines our technological situa-tion, much more than the scientific research projects that we (somewhat naively) see as feeding directly into new tools, like the magician conjuring a new alchemical potion out of thin air, having expended nothing but time. What is more, we can measure our depth into cyberg existence by looking at the numbers of people and things involved in the cybernetic network. A hammer made a millennia ago involved a miner and a blacksmith, a mule and a horse, a mine, a furnace and trees; no more than about a hundred beings and things were entailed in this early cyberg example. A functionally identical hammer today would entail a network of ten thousand beings and things, or even a hundred thousand.

Our cybergs get bigger, deeper, wider, and as they do our autonomy *recedes* even while the imagined scope of our autonomy grows. This is part of the technological blindness I have previously called 'cyberfetish' and am here marking as shallow-sightedness – our strange capacity to see only the powers and potentials of our new tools, but to overlook or underjudge their consequences. Precisely because we have moved away from tools that could be made by individuals or villages, to tools that require nations or corporations to build and maintain, we live at a time where the cyberg is the measure of both possibility and catastrophe.

Although I have introduced the idea of a cyberg through the extended frameworks behind a specific tool, the concept behind these cybernetic meshes applies whenever beings and things are linked together into extended networks. When Benedict Anderson observed that the printing press allowed the imagined communities we call nations to form, his argument can be read as saying that *nations are cybergs*. Every corporation is a cyberg, constituted slightly differently from nations, but in the last half-century rivalling and exceeding them for power and influence. Every one of us is embroiled and imbricated in cybernetic networks of such scope and influence as to make a mockery of our mythos of technological empowerment. For when it comes to our tools, the enhancement of our personal agency is truly just the tip of the cyberg.

Scaling Our Cybernetic Networks

Every purposeful network of beings and things forms a cyberg, where (like an iceberg) we only see a fraction of the entailed network and the rest lurks beyond our awareness most of the time. It is possible to investigate further (actor-network theory is precisely a method for doing so), but encyclopaedic knowledge is an unreasonable expectation for such complex and multi-faceted manifolds. While the complete inventory of beings and things entailed within each of these cybernetic networks would be challenging to enumerate, we can approximate the *scale* of each cyberg by counting just the number of one kind of entity within it, e.g. the number of humans, the number of computers.

In attempting to judge the scale of specific cybergs, I have constrained my attention to those networks that span their entire breadth with some kind of active relation, even if merely one of potential. A nation is a good example: not every citizen knows every other citizen, yet they are linked by a shared bureaucracy that integrates them all into one functional network. It is not enough for there to have been a common network of production – no matter how many people own a penknife, penknife-wielders do not have any ongoing relationship. Conversely, both through licensing records and the requirement for the further purchasing of ammunition, a firearm has an active relation, even if it is sometimes merely a potential relationship. Even if there are a few gun owners who never buy ammo, the network that distributes bullets still remains.

In some cases, the immediate cybergs involved are relatively local in organisation, but these regional cybernetic networks have their own shared relationships at a more global scale, thus making them collectively into a larger-scale cyberg. For example, while individual television stations are modestly-sized cybergs by contemporary standards, the exchange of broadcast media effectively links TV stations and their viewers globally such that they aggregate into something far more substantial. (Religions are something of a borderline case in this regard, but I shall set these aside for now.)

In the discussion that follows, I want to discuss some key contemporary cybergs in terms of the quantity of a single indexed entity, either humans or devices. We can use the metric system's Greek-derived prefixes to distinguish between *kilocybergs* (with thousands of entities sufficiently involved to count as being within the network), *megacybergs* (with millions), and *gigacybergs* (with billions or, in what is now called the long scale, thousands of millions). My primary interest will be the ten largest networks, the gigacybergs, with no fewer than a billion entities embroiled in their networks. These categorisations are not intended to be definitive but merely indicative – they point to the general situation today from a perspective we would not normally consider.

A number of megacybergs narrowly missed out on inclusion in my 'top ten' examples of largest cybergs, including: the European Union (743 million people involved), the film industry (about 800 million participating people), and firearms (around 875 million gun owners). More than 360,000 people die each year as a result of the gun cyberg, and yet this is by no means the most fatal of our cybernetic networks. It is also worth mentioning that if the informal rankings that follow included the major world religions, Christianity would be the number three gigacyberg (2.3 billion), Islam would be ranked jointly with Microsoft (1.5 billion), and the Hindu traditions would be a close runner up (900 million). I leave it as an exercise for the reader to establish the significance, if any, of these particular numbers.

In joint ninth place among the gigacybergs, we have Chinese internet giant Tencent and search colossus Google, both having about a billion humans in their cyberg. Whereas Tencent does not lead China's internet search providers (that honour goes to Baidu) it has a tremendously diverse network of internet services, including the wildly successful competitive game service *League of Legends*. Google dominates search globally – but even this only allows it to squeak into the world's biggest cybergs, if we take its quoted figures as accurately gauging its scale. Pragmatically, the reach of the Google cyberg is probably greater than this conservative estimate – but it feels somehow fitting to show this young upstart beginning its climb towards the top of the heap...

Next, in eighth place, we have the 1.2 billion automobiles that form the car gigacyberg. It is possible to drive completely around the world thanks to the extent that the car-human cyborg has emerged as the dominant lifeform on our planet. We have completely changed the ecology of almost every ecological biome by installing the infrastructure required to make cars a viable form of transportation, and we entirely ignore the colossal impact of this situation on a daily basis. This is the world's deadliest cyberg, taking more than 1.25 million human lives annually, and that figure does not include war deaths some would attribute to the oil industry that feeds this network.

At seventh and sixth, we have India and China, with 1.3 and 1.4 billion humans respectively. These are the only nations to qualify for this 'top ten' list, and each has more than four times the population of the United States, and nearly twice the population of the European Union. China is the wealthier cyberg, with an economy four times the size of India's, but both wield significant destructive power via their hundreds of nuclear weapons. However, they have less than 2.5% of the world's nuclear stockpile, since the US and the Russian Federation hold 45% and 48% of the world's nuclear weapons, a quantity far beyond any rational consideration. The relatively poor showing of nations in this 'countdown' is a sign of our times: our planet is no longer dominated by the national cybergs, even though they remain powerful, influential, and ubiquitous.

Microsoft claims the number five spot, being slightly larger than our most populous nations at about 1.5 billion robots. Despite no longer being the centre of attention in technology circles, Microsoft's cyberg is 50% bigger than the certifiable size of Google's, thanks to the continuing dominance of Windows, which has a 90% market share in desktops and laptops. That said, these are now only 20% of the robot market, which is dominated by smartphones (where Google enjoys 87% of the market). Microsoft is a cyberg in decline, unable to adequately break into the marketplace for robots that fit in our pockets, yet it still jealously guards its hold over other industrial cybergs.

Just slightly ahead in terms of scale is the fourth-place gigacyberg, television, with about 1.6 billion humans watching a TV set for entertainment, news, sports coverage and so forth. That TV enjoys only a marginal numerical advantage over Microsoft is a sign of how completely the computer has positioned itself as the cybernetic successor to the notorious boob tube. Yet there is another lesson here: the television is *not* ubiquitous, being a cyberg that extends through only 20% of our planet's human population. It is hard to say whether we should judge this as a cyberg in decline, or whether (as might be a fairer assessment) this is becoming just one more medium incorporated into the internet.

Facebook claims the bronze medal with its two billion humans. Here again we get a sense of the power of the digital cybergs; it has taken a little over a decade for Facebook to become the first definitive 'double billionaire' cybernetic network owned by a single corporate entity. By leveraging our social instincts – and largely by accident, for it was not originally designed to operate as a surrogate for human relationships – Facebook has aggregated more humans into one walled garden than anything else.

I have awarded second place to the internet, with its 3.5 billion humans. It is distributed, beyond outright control (but certainly open to influence), and the largest electronic cyberg on our planet. The internet is so significant, most dictionaries think it deserves a capital letter, like a nation. This is a cyberg on a scale beyond national bureaucracies, a network that links half the planet's humans to almost all the planet's computers. Cisco claims there were 8.7 billion devices connected to the internet in 2012. As cybergs go, this one is the most spectacular in scale and potential. Yet it is still arguably outstripped by at least one larger cyberg: *money*.

It was the first cybernetic network, the first technical system to spread around our planet as both practice and tacit relations, and I estimate some 7.3 billion humans are enmeshed in this apex gigacyberg. As humans have grown more populous, so too has money spread with us – including into the virtual spaces of the internet, where this cyberg now lives, as much or more than it does in the pockets of its humans. It seems positively simplistic next to the other gigacybergs, yet it engulfs almost every human; I have estimated that only 1-2% of the population of our planet are not caught up in the commercial cybernetic system.

The sheer ubiquity of money as a concept is so complete that politics hinges more around budgetary numbers than about questions of how to live. This is one of our first technologies, as old as civilisation – and it remains our most successful. In the previous chapter, I warned about the cyber-domination of our robots, but how much worse is this risk in the context of our financial games? Money maintains its power because we all accept it has value, and thus any human can exchange money with almost any other human for almost any conceivable purpose. This is our greatest and most overbearing cybernetic network, the ultimate expression of the domination of things. Who can honestly say they have never been forced into submission by money?

Beyond Futile Outrage

Seeing our situation from the perspective of these vast cybernetic networks transforms our viewpoint on what is going on. We are habituated to treating all the nations as equivalent entities, all the corporations as another kind of thing, and we do not consider tools as in any way equivalent to either. But as cybergs, all these disparate networks share both scale and influence upon our lives, and understanding the human condition as the cyborg's condition within its cybergs is to move from Enlightenment thinking – where humans were the point of equality, and the sole source of agency – to something radically different.

This is the age we live in. Call it what you will, and there are many choices ('anthropocene' seems popular, sadly), the Age of Distraction combines the capacity for gigacybergs to radically reconfigure the planet we live upon with the slow recognition that *we do not have control*. Or, perhaps more accurately, *nothing is in control*, least of all humanity: we cannot even advance productive discussions since our only shared points of reference are our flesh and the money it serves, robots and their internet, and (perhaps...) having a Facebook page. We do not adequately understand our situation as cyborgs enmeshed within cybergs, and until we can bring this into focus we lack any viable method of bringing about a lasting change in our circumstances. This shallow-sightedness is effectively a cyber-debility and to be deep-sighted its corresponding cybervirtue.

This brings us to a paradox about contemporary cy-

borg existence: the internet seems to be overflowing with outrage, yet nothing changes. A key part of this problem is that
when our moral intuitions provoke us to anger, we voice our
hatred or cynicism online and somehow feel that is enough;
the itch has been scratched. Nothing changes, because the last
common ethical backdrop we shared was the one that came
about through the Enlightenment, which ended roughly two
centuries ago. Over the intervening time we have lost the
common ground that made the ethical thought of this movement so powerful. The human is no longer the measure of all
things and religion is no longer as effective at uniting moral
intuitions thanks to our chaotic nova of alternative perspectives. Sustained discussion now seems impossible in politics
(which has become a sport), in academia (which has become a
ritualised echo chamber) or the news (which has become entertainment).

Within the chaos nova, we are somewhat adrift. We
have lost a common ethical backdrop against which we can
adequately even discuss our ethics, let alone bring about any
kind of change. Our moral intuitions have lost their force,
since the context that gave them meaning has broken down.
As the earlier discussion of cyber-kindness brought into focus,
the result is anger against other people who do not share our
values with no possibility of a productive dialogue that can
bring about a new state of affairs. Moral horror traps us. The
absence of tactful ways to overcome the cultural collisions of
the internet generates little more than rage against the inade-
quacies of everyone else to meet our own expectations. This is
the paralysis brought on by outrage culture.

To bring about changes requires a common standard,
and the problem with contemporary ethical thought is that we
do not understand our moral mythos well enough to maintain

a shared basis for judgement. As moral psychologists have reported, the tendency is for us to have an emotional response
to a situation (e.g. outrage), then afterwards to dress it up in
justifications (e.g. demonisation of a particular identity) – social psychologist Jonathan Haidt waggishly dubbed this 'the
emotional dog and his rational tail'. However, I break with
the psychologists who advance this theory at the conclusions
they draw from it, which amount to the perilous assumption
that moral philosophy has no viable role. Furthermore, I question some of their research methods, which are inadequate to
many of the conclusions being drawn.

Haidt's idea, for example, that our moral intuitions
are embedded in our social connections, is substantially correct. However, it is not significantly contra to the views of
any philosopher, as many academics have pointed out. What's
missing in Haidt's social intuitionist model is how the social
intuitions became set up: he has forgotten the role of history
in establishing common standards of moral judgement, and
once this is taken into account it becomes clear that contemporary morality is intimately connected to moral philosophy.
Indeed, as moral and political philosopher Alasdair MacIntyre
outlined thirty-five years ago in his influential book, *After Virtue*, the nature of this moral catastrophe is the lack of connection between our habits of judgement and their philosophical
roots, which can be traced across the span of European history. Attempting to remove philosophy from consideration, as
key moral psychologists such as Haidt argue, is to deepen the
crisis, not resolve it, and Haidt ultimately ends up advancing
an impotent argument for the status quo. We will get nowhere
if we fail to situate the ethical crisis within its cultural history.

The three key approaches to morality are concerned
with the qualities of agents (virtue), the nature of actions

(duty), and the consequences that result (outcomes). I contend that all three forms of moral thinking are vital, but it is important to remember that for the majority of the recorded history of our species, the concept of virtue has been the primary vehicle of morality. Whatever grasp individuals may or may not have had of their wider situation, the idea that it is a good thing to be brave, polite, patient, generous, or kind was easy to grasp – even if it was not always so easy to put into practice.

MacIntyre's *After Virtue* traces the history of virtues up to their contemporary near-demise, supplanted by two new moral systems devised in the Enlightenment. Firstly, Kant's duty-based philosophy leads to human rights, but then inexplicably devolves into posturing about 'having a right' in situations where nothing of the kind applies. (Here, Haidt is right: moral philosophy is not entailed in people's moral judgements: but in such cases that is *precisely* the problem.) Secondly, John Stuart Mill's outcome-based utilitarianism begins by aiming at 'maximising the good' yet leads to contemporary corporate consequentialism that merely maximises profit. Consequentialism risks thinking only of the end point of a method: to think only outcomes matter, not means. This is understandable, given the emphasis people naturally place on 'how things turn out', but it can dangerously flatten how we think about moral problems. What's more, these kinds of consequentialism, which judge purely by outcome, are systems that no longer resemble morality at all, as the late Derek Parfit accused.

Thus we are beset by moral disasters, as we have all but lost one of our methods for thinking about ethics, and broken the others such that otherwise laudable moral systems have become corrupted distortions of themselves. This is the nature of the two major disasters of contemporary ethics – the *moral disaster of individualism*, which confuses selfishness or paternalism for collective responsibility, and the *moral disaster of consequentialism*, which boils down complex situations to the point that decisions are easy to make, and in the process destroys the essential context of every ethical challenge. Remember these twin moral disasters, as they will recur throughout the rest of the book.

In terms of the disaster of individualism, there is an urgent need to repair our broken concepts of rights now that nations such as the United States and the United Kingdom have abandoned them, while individuals still angrily invoke 'their rights' without any understanding of what that claim implies. There is an even more vital requirement to reconfigure the kind of consequentialist thinking that leads both nations and corporations to act in appalling ways because their definitions of what is good is reduced to the merely calculable – substituting expediency for any concept of ethics. Neither of these recovery projects has much hope of success without a substantial reboot of moral thinking, and the academic community cannot achieve this – not without engaging with the wider populace it has been regrettably isolated from through a myopic faith that the truth emerges from fighting under the cloak of anonymity.

Outrage culture is the product of people who project morality against others, and rarely use it to judge themselves. There is a natural tendency to do this that has been well known by philosophers and indeed religious teachers for many centuries. What is conspicuously absent today in this regard is shared reflection on our ethical values and judgements, something also suggested as necessary by Haidt's social intuitionist theory. We need to represent our moral positions to each other in part because once our anger is engaged, productive discussion is blocked by moral horror, and so the reflective aspect of morality – which is far more important than we usually recognise – never occurs. If there is a lesson we should take from moral psychology it is not that we should abandon the study of our historically embedded moral systems but that we have failed to adequately maintain the social basis of moral judgement. We are no longer conducting any viable form of morality, and we really have become the caricature Haidt imagines, dressing up our emotional reactions in convenient justifications.

To overcome this impasse requires new discourses, and it is my suggestion that we start by talking about virtues (as I am doing here in this book) since we can recognise what is good in a person – or a cyborg – without it setting off our moral horror, which closes us off from difficult-to-accept ideas. Too much of our ethical practice has become a sustained outpouring of vitriol against what we perceive as evil, often without ever stopping to consider the complexities of the situations. Whether we are talking about those who voted to leave the EU in the United Kingdom or those who voted for a populist demagogue in the United States, it is not enough to angrily cry 'racism! racism!' and expect this to suffice as politics – or ethics. Perhaps if we can recover some perspective on the *good*, we can stop being ineffectually obsessed with raging at the evil we see everywhere around us.

If there is a way forward from here – and I would not be writing this book if I did not think it possible – it entails changes to the way we think about both morality and ourselves. We have to recognise that we are cyborgs, and that we depend in turn upon our cybergs. All of the cybernetic networks around us – including those underpinning our use of robots, the internet, and even money – have a substantial effect upon us and our planet, and many of the consequences of this situation are impossible to bring into focus because we are shallow-sighted. Even if we ignore virtue and cybervirtue as ways of thinking about this, we would have to recognise that there was a problem – indeed, many problems – that need to be addressed if we want to be a species with any kind of a future ahead of us in the long term.

The twin moral disasters of individualism and consequentialism have come about because the ethical systems that appeared in the Enlightenment as alternatives to thinking in terms of virtue have inadvertently destroyed the basis for any viable morality. Kant and the other Enlightenment thinkers, who brought about a radical new focus upon individual freedom, could not have conceived that the empowerment of the individual would lead to the moral disaster of individualism. Mill and the utilitarians that followed him wanted to 'maximize the good', but this honourable (if implausible) goal has devolved into the moral disaster of consequentialism that merely substitutes calculation for moral reflection. We need a shared perspective on justice and the good life, bound together by common practices. It is this we lack, without even realising it is missing.

Outrage culture is either impotent or blindly vengeful, indulging in cyber-cruelty and then spuriously justifying it as the pursuit of justice. Neither of these situations are terribly helpful. What we encounter in the clashes of the internet is the shallow-sightedness of the cyborg confronted with the immeasurable scope of the cybergs they are enmeshed within, occurring in the context of our unrecognised moral cybernetic networks. These fossilised remnants of Enlightenment religion and philosophy are incapable of bringing about change because they have become utterly divorced from any lived practices. Without a shared understanding of 'the good life' we never quite know what is right, we are just certain that *the others have it wrong*. To get beyond this, we have to learn to practice morality in ways that can cross easily between any religious or secular tradition, and virtues might just provide a way of doing this. Yet truly overcoming our stalemate might require something more than this. We may have to rediscover what it means to stay faithful to something.

V. FIDELITY

*Fidelity is the virtue that aids commitment to practices
and their communities. In a robot, cyber-fidelity is the – possibly
hypothetical! – quality that would encourage this without engendering
any additional dependence upon the robot itself. In this chapter,
I consider what has gone wrong with our understanding of fidelity,
and how recovering a sense of the importance of this virtue could
improve conviviality, which is Ivan Illich's term for societies where
technology supports interrelated people. Illich's idea of 'convivial
tools' might just be a clue to finding how robots and cyborgs
might display cyber-fidelity.*

High Tech, Low Fidelity

The virtue of fidelity is perhaps the hardest idea for anyone
to appreciate in this age of robots. The concept of faithfulness
and loyalty to a person, cause, or ideal feels like a relic from
a time before our own, and attempts to espouse the merits
of this otherwise simple concept flounder on the twin moral
calamities we face. This question is parallel to the ambiguity
over when persistence and determination constitutes a virtue.
Indeed, fidelity and tenacity are closely-related virtues – one
binds us to an ideal, a practice, or a community, the other to
a course of action. Understanding why fidelity is something
valuable – indeed, invaluable – means defending against the
twin catastrophic corruptions of ethical life that have afflict-
ed our time and showing how both are rooted in abandoning
fidelity for something lesser. Yet before it can be argued that
fidelity is worthwhile, we must recognise that we currently
lack it and appreciate how this came about.

A brief warning is required. When we enter the fault-lines of our ways of thinking, it can be difficult to remain open to new perspectives. Moral horror makes it hard to even listen to a new perspective that strikes us as beyond belief. Thus to talk about fidelity and freedom in the paradoxical way I am about to is likely to set in motion all manner of resistances. Objections will loom large and make it easy to miss the point I am trying to make. By all means consider the arguments against what I am presenting; I would expect no less. But always leave open the possibility that no matter what I may have got wrong, there might be an essential truth at the heart of my argument worth grasping.

To understand the subtle problem I wish to outline, we must be able to appreciate the cybernetic networks (or cybergs) that we are enmeshed within and how they relate to the moral catastrophes of our time. Consider first the disaster of individualism that tells us that we only have to be loyal to ourselves, and celebrates breaking free of tradition as a triumph of the individual will. There are indeed situations worth celebrating here, and movies like *Footloose* and *Bend It Like Beckham* rely upon this for their drama: parents enforcing religious standards bar their children from behaving in certain ways. Yet these stories serve to re-illuminate Christian and Sikh practices; *Footloose* is as much a lesson for Christians as it is a celebration of individual freedom, and while Sikh traditions are a less relevant part of *Bend It Like Beckham*, the same general point remains.

Conversely, individualist doctrine serves to valorise *any* exit from religious traditions as a victory for freedom. Yet this escape is of the most fragmentary kind: those who make a clean break from their family and its locally-social network merely transfer from one small cyberg into the dispersed gigacybergs that absorb us all. Without ties to other practices, those founded upon people, the result is a chimerical existence as a free individual, one whose freedom consists solely in the choices of consumption being placed before us. This is the disaster of individualism at its core: we say we value individuality, yet foster a way of living that sacrifices any more substantial freedom in favour of merely pre-prescribed market decisions.

We have misunderstood 'liberty' as 'individual choice', and in so doing have lost any grasp over authentic freedom. This mistake is so subtly concealed from view that our typical understanding of our situation is the inverse of what a closer examination reveals. We think that breaking free of the traditions and practices of our parents or extended family is the mark of freedom because we remove from our lives an influence that seems to impede our autonomy. Yet the core practices of both individual and group remain the same after this alleged 'split'. We are still embedded within the cybernetic networks of money, digital media, medicine, cars, and transportation – the spaces where we are assured of our individuality through participation with a common culture of movies, games, scientific discovery, news and so forth. This shared background tells us we are free because we can change job and move to a new city – that we are free, in other words, because we are nomads, unbound from tradition.

Except, of course, for the traditions of money, media, medicine, technology, and transportation, which are (in the case of money) as old as the religious traditions that it is supposedly an expression of freedom to break with. The point being that we have equated our capacity for infidelity as freedom because we do not see any expression of liberty in

the possibility of disentangling ourselves from the various cybergs that enclose us. Moreover, *we do not even see that possibility
at all*. It is entirely beyond our thought.

Within the cybernetic networks that enfold us, we
possess only the minimum freedom of choice within a closed
market, never the mark of authentic freedom that would
come from the liberty to disengage from the cyberg itself.
The matter of the car makes this clear: please, choose which
motorized vehicle you wish to use to participate in transportation. Effectively, you *must* do so if you are not to be radically
disadvantaged by being unable to move around in the ways
required by our planetary infrastructure. It is, paradoxically,
only the human who lives *outside* the road network who possesses an authentic freedom of movement, which is to say, the
capacity to move in *any direction*. The physical nomadism of
the Tuareg shows a genuine personal freedom when measured
against the cultural nomadism of the city-dweller, who claims
their infidelity as freedom, while having no choice but to engage in transportation, money, and so forth.

Yet this is done willingly; it does not seem like a lack
of choice because accepting all of these enmeshing networks is
clearly desirable to us all, since the values by which we gauge
our decisions to participate are taken to be beyond question.
This is the moral disaster of consequentialism: we know unequivocally that outcomes matter (this is beyond doubt), and
thus *utility* – the capacity to bring about desired outcomes –
is the yardstick of all choices. Who could doubt that better
technology is more useful than the tools remaining the same,
or that living longer is better than dying young, or that getting between two points faster is better than doing so slower,
or that superior entertainment beats boredom? Who could
doubt that more money is better than less?

We weigh outcomes and think that this is the measure that cannot be doubted. But when this is the only way we evaluate things, we are being shallow-sighted. Yes, once we level transportation down to mere time between points, it's a relatively simple question of what is better. Yet this hides the way roads replace other, more egalitarian spaces; how pedestrians and cyclists must choose between going further or gambling with their lives; how both the cost and the impact of living is raised by mandatory car ownership. Do we want to give up cars? Probably not. But we ought to look at them more closely than measuring them by expense, fuel consumption, and speed. You don't just buy a car, you buy into the automotive infrastructure that the car requires to work. You buy into the car's cyberg and all that entails, every submerged aspect that is buried beneath the imagined ideal of faster, further travel and the fantasy of driving conveyed by automobile commercials. A higher top speed won't get you to your destination any sooner when you spend most of your journey stuck in traffic, as cities are learning far too slowly.

So too in medicine: no-one can look at the frequency that women died in childbirth just a century or so ago, nor the number of children that perished as mere babes, and not feel compelled to criticise those who, for instance, refuse vaccinations that benefit everyone. But again, we are shallow-sighted with medicine. The medical establishment causes almost as many problems as it cures, not least of which because this view of life – as permanently extensible with the right tools – sets us up for certain failure. The developed world's seemingly unlimited abilities in healthcare leads us into certain patterns of thinking, asking that we identify every problem as a disease, research a cure, and administer all cures to all people.

Yet this is an ever-increasing task, becoming more and more expensive and either distributing the best healthcare only to the wealthy, or gradually bankrupting nations that attempt to pay for everything, for everyone. Do we want to give up medicine? Absolutely not. But still, we shall all eventually die, and medicine does not help us deal with that inevitability – it is rather our most effective way of hiding from it.

Money is the subtlest trap of them all, because the idea that more money is better is so effective at concealing the radical unimportance of money to well-being. This is not the same as saying poverty is great – by definition, those living in poverty don't have enough. But what standard do we aim for? The moment you are living inside the car cyberg, your cost of living just skyrocketed because transportation is taken as expected for each individual instead of – as humans once took for granted – as a community good. You no longer need just food and shelter, now you need a car too. And the more money you have, the worse it becomes... second houses, sports cars, private jets – expense rises to match income, ensuring dissatisfaction. Worse still, the large accumulations of money become cybergs all of their own: capital chases its tail in a game of perpetual commercial deployment that has little benefit to anyone but the venture capitalists playing with the networks of extreme wealth.

Now the point here is not the critique of these specific cybergs – although there are dozens of unthought-of, undiscussed problems and crises hidden just beneath the surface. It is that our supposed expressions of individualism – breaking from tradition, leaving the family business, moving to another city or country – do not adequately represent personal freedom since whether we stay within or break away from our childhood culture, we remain inside all the gigacyberg networks of our time.

This is not even a new critique. Ivan Illich outlined these problems (albeit from a different perspective) in the 1970s. He observed that the industrialised world had imposed what he termed *radical monopolies* that eliminated meaningful alternatives in certain contexts. We call it a monopoly when one corporation has exclusive control over the market for a certain commodity or service. A radical monopoly is where one *kind* of commodity or service has exclusive control over the satisfaction of a certain need. Cars are an excellent example: most contemporary cities have built their infrastructure on the assumption of the automobile as the primary means of transportation, excluding more egalitarian means of transport, such as bicycles. Almost fifty years on from Illich's critique, and we are still beset by radical monopolies, dominating systems that replace freedom with choices set upon their own rigid terms.

Christian, Hindu, atheist, Sikh, Buddhist, pagan, Muslim... all these supposedly distinct belief systems are taking part in the same practices – technology and all its messy consequences. No matter how you try to break with your parent's practices, at the same time you continue the medical, transportational, commercial practices that you acquired *from your parents*. Thus, individualism is in crisis. Not because it is wrong to want to be free, but because we say we are free merely because we can vary the minutiae of our lives and beliefs, and do not recognise how the common basis of evaluation remains unchanged. Individualism destroys fidelity because ultimately it is unbreakably allied to consequentialism in its narrow guise of utility.

High technology, low fidelity. We always go for the better, the new, a taste of the future over loyalty to the past.

We do so because we are *cultural nomads*, and we have all chosen to live in essentially the same ways – not out of loyalty, but out of a bitter necessity born of our dependence upon the cybergs towards which we cannot even claim fidelity. For how can we be faithful to something that we cannot even imagine the possibility of leaving?

The twin disasters of individualism and consequentialism are catastrophic precisely because they distort our understanding of everything; from the technological systems we all share in, to the families and cultural backgrounds that are unique to our personal circumstances. These disastrous misunderstandings create the impression that breaking from tradition is the most authentic form of individual expression, despite the fact that breaking from tradition actually requires the abandonment of a rather large part of what makes us individual: our unique circumstances. Whatever identity we take on after such a conscious break, the majority of our situation – the networks of technology we live within – remains entirely unchanged.

Faith in What?

High technology has crippled the virtue of fidelity by ensuring that it is only ever practiced as the thoughtless failure to recognise how little freedom we possess with respect to the technological traditions within which we are enmeshed. But it is still necessary to understand why fidelity is a virtue; why loyalty to people, practices, and ideals serves a vital purpose in human life, without which our capacity for judgement is impaired. But this requires first a change in our understanding of faith.

One place to start is marriage, but not because everyone accepts the merits of this institution. Indeed, before same-sex marriage managed to put this practice back on the agenda in a significant and hopefully lasting way, I feared matrimony was to be the latest casualty of the homogenisation of contemporary life. While there is a host of feminist (and more recently, male-advocacy) arguments against marriage, I do not intend to engage with these because they have little day-to-day force. Moreover, if a feminist or anti-feminist eschews marriage on principle, I see this as merely a new form of monastic commitment founded on political rather than religious grounds. You are not bound to adhere to what any gender advocate thinks, which is not the same as saying their arguments don't matter.

The people around me in long-term relationships who are not wed are what I only half-jokingly call *unmarried*, a term parallel to the word 'undead', used for imaginary beings that are neither dead nor alive. These unhusbands and unwives put forward more-or-less the same arguments against marriage: *we don't need the government to validate our relationship; a ring on our fingers changes nothing; what would a wedding ceremony do except cost a lot of money?* All these objections miss the core purpose of marriage in a society of equals: to make, as equals, a public commitment to building a life together. The act of promising is the key to matrimony, because it is, in a very real sense, the marriage. It is both the act of committing, which forms a particular kind of relationship between individuals and their futures, and the witnessing of this act that constitutes the wedding, thus founding the marriage. You don't necessarily need to get married in front of your families – but if you cannot present your future spouse to those with whom you have prior long-term relationships, how serious about your promise are you?

A promise, whether public or private, is the basis of

fidelity. It is not coincidental that having extramarital sex is called 'infidelity'; it is a breaking of vows, of faith in the other – hence also 'unfaithful'. The very word comes to us as faith, *fides* in Latin. We have also come to associate the word 'faith' with religion, thanks to the Protestant doctrine of *sola fide*, but this need not concern us here. The important point is that faith, as a trust that cannot be unequivocally vindicated, is an essential aspect of human experience, and we lose sight of this if we buy into the mythos of 'faith versus reason', which stages a battle between faith in tradition and faith in the sciences that is spectacularly unhelpful for understanding either.

Thinking that continued scientific research will only make the world better is to have blind faith in the sciences; it is neither testable, nor at this time even entirely plausible, that this is the case. But we have faith in the sciences because we contrast what we have to what our ancestors had, and judge it better, and by this isolated measure we seem to be vindicated. The equivalent 'blind faith' in tradition occurs when faith, which is a disposition towards uncertainty, becomes equated with unjustified certainty – all too often with disastrous results. In almost any situation, *blind* faith is a debility, since instead of the balance of faith and critical thinking, it substitutes rigid conviction – and balance is required to negotiate the difficulties of future uncertainties. In matrimony, this blind faith can be seen when one partner ceases to be actively engaged in the endless negotiation of a shared life and merely assumes that the marriage will continue. This is not having 'faith' in your partner at all, but is rather a painful path towards divorce.

It is because the future is *always* uncertain that faith is an unavoidable aspect of human life. Rather than recognising this, we find ways to hide from it by highlighting things that feel beyond doubt and pretending that faith is a character flaw of others. The moral disaster of consequentialism, reducing all judgements to questions of utility, is a crucial example of this since it obscures manifest problems by setting them entirely outside of consideration. The question of how useful a certain tool might be will ultimately prove irrelevant to a species that has destroyed its environment to the point of risking its own extinction.

Yet if this catastrophe comes too keenly into our attention, it becomes depressing. It robs us of our will to act, because our apparent powerlessness against the most serious problems of our time diminishes our sense of autonomy, and thus our willingness to even *attempt* to act. Against this paralysing impotence, the only possible bulwark is faith — and in this context it almost doesn't matter what that faith is vested in, as long as it bolsters our capacity for effective action rather than merely comforting or entertaining us into accepting the status quo. Levi Bryant recently argued for an outcome-focussed ethics concerned with the fragility of the future of 'bodies' (organisms, organisations, nations...). These futures are the ones we construct for ourselves out of what we deem they ought to be — and to be able to imagine such futures requires a faith in *what could be*.

Yet 'faith' in this sense is not fidelity, but merely the background required to understand it. Returning to the example of marriage, fidelity does not necessarily mean abstaining from sex with others besides your spouse. Depending upon the vows that were taken, even this is not necessarily excluded from fidelity, for all that it might be generally safer to do so. Fidelity means keeping the faith of the vow that was taken, which, in the memorable phrasing of the Christian ceremony means to keep the faith against all adversity: 'for richer, for poorer, in sickness and in health'. Thus fidelity marks the sustaining of faith against the ever-changing turbulence of life. Aristotle suggested that for every virtue there was a debility caused by lack of it, and another for having *too much* – for fidelity, blind faith is the debility of excess, and faithlessness its absence.

There is another sense of fidelity that is important here. A recording is said to be 'high fidelity' (from which we get 'hi-fi') when it accurately reproduces the audio quality of the original music. We then call the resulting recording a 'faithful reproduction' of the original event. Fidelity in this sense is a relationship between past, present, and future – what happened in the past is reproduced in the present, and reproducible in the future. And this is *also* the sense in which fidelity applies in all other cases too, if perhaps with a less draconian standard of exactitude to qualify as 'faithful'. For the spouse who does not cheat upon their partner and avoids infidelity, this means that there is a fidelity between the past (the vow), and the present and future that follow from it. Fidelity is thus continuity, constancy, loyalty. It is to make a leap of faith into the future and to then remain true to the meaning of that prior event.

Now there is an important challenge here: how do you know what you should be giving your fidelity to? Alain Badiou, a philosopher for whom fidelity to an event of truth is the very essence of morality, is keen to stress the disasters that will occur if we pledge ourselves to something which is not true. This, to his critics, makes him no better than the Christian existentialist Søren Kierkegaard, who challenged us to be true to ourselves in the face of the absurd, which he identified with God. The twentieth century existentialists removed God from the equation, and thus shook free any standard that might allow us to know with any confidence what was true.

This inadvertently collapsed the Enlightenment philosophy of equality into the disaster of individualism. Like the existentialists, Badiou denies God – albeit by a bizarre recourse to mathematics ('the one is not') – yet wants to hold on to Kierkegaard's divine truth all the same. Can he?

Between Kierkegaard's existentialism and Badiou's 'ethic of truths' lies a range of encounters with events that might invite people to exercise fidelity. The question of how we know whether something is deserving of our faith is, surprisingly, not as important as it seems, for *having* faith and *falling into* blind faith are not the same thing. It is tragic that practitioners of religion often confuse the two, and ironic that opponents of tradition can make the same kind of mistake. Faith and certainty are opposing concepts, even though they come from essentially the same source, differing primarily in degree. It would not be a leap of faith if we could be certain about something, and the future is the one thing that could not, *could never* be certain. It is always fragile. It is precisely that fragility that can only be combated by fidelity.

This presents a radical challenge to our understanding of freedom, one entirely opposed to the implausible idea that breaking from tradition is the hallmark of freedom. On the contrary, maintaining the practices of a tradition – whether religious, scientific, artistic, or personal – involves honouring the freedom that was involved in the original commitment to that tradition, whenever that occurred. Of course, if such a promise was never made, that is a different matter – blindly accepting every tradition you encounter is hardly virtuous. But fidelity, in marriage or any other kind of sustained practice, is an essential virtue if we are not to give up our authentic individuality and merely conform to the common networks of technology that we all share.

The Dependent World

Either the dog is the paragon of fidelity, expressing bound-less loyalty to their human, or dogs are incapable of fidelity. It comes down to whether the bond a dog forms with their pack leader counts as a promise – there are good reasons to say that it doesn't. Nonetheless, I come down firmly on the side of the former argument and see dogs as practicing fidelity in their own unique and admirable way. The counter-argument amounts to claiming a dog's commitment is merely instinctual habit. And it is in this contrast, of habit against fidelity, that we cyborgs are encountering our most serious problems.

In *Imaginary Games*, I draw against Félix Ravaisson's remarkable 1838 conception of 'habit' as the trait that sets liv-ing beings aside from things. Habit, for Ravaisson, has two sides – it is the foundation of all our skills and excellences, which are only transformed into concrete achievements through the repetition of training and application. Yet it is also the source of addiction, and it is not coincidental that phrases such as 'habitual user' and 'habit-forming' are attached to substances such as heroin. The virtue of fidelity that I have been carefully tracing is that which allows our skills to achieve their excellence – as when the artisan, artist, athlete, or re-searcher achieves proficiency through commitment to their chosen path. This may well entail tenacity, but that term im-plies pursuit of a specific goal: it is fidelity, rather than tenac-ity, that truly binds us to a practice for long enough that we can achieve a degree of mastery.

These activities that become more reliable through their exercise, and that are shared by some kind of communi-ty, are *practices*. All skills and competences can be understood as practices, and this includes even moral competences such as virtues. In fact, 'knowledge' itself is not a bucket of facts held in the head, but is demonstrated in practices. There is authentic knowledge in any practice that can be performed with a degree of reliability and that allows for the assertion of facts as a side effect of its execution. This is obvious, when you think about it – anyone can learn to recite the times tables, but knowledge entails understanding how they are made and why they make sense.

All knowledge is a practice: the baker knows how to make bread, the artist knows how to sketch what they see, the high-jumper knows how to clear the bar, and the micro-biologist knows how to work a microscope to identify a bacterium. In all these cases, knowing is never merely repeating facts – it always entails being able to do something, and that competence is attained solely by habit, by the repetition that fosters excellence, which makes an activity into a skill. Whoever can do these things *also* knows the facts concerning their relevant practice. When we, for instance, 'know' that yeast is used to make bread, this is 'known' only in the most trivial sense if we do not actually have the knowledge that comes from being able to bake bread. If this argument is accepted, this means *all knowledge comes from fidelity*, since if knowledge is understood as a practice, only fidelity to a practice attains it.

Whenever we exercise fidelity, these practices bond us with other people. There is a hidden aspect to this that I tried to draw attention to before by taking marriage as an exemplar of the difference between faith (which can be blind) and fidelity (sustaining the true meaning of the original vow). The fact that fidelity bonds us is perhaps most visible in the example of marriage, but it can be found in all cases in which fidelity occurs (even if it is sometimes a commitment to honour the dead in some way, rather than the living). The artisan's fidelity to their craft binds them both to those that they learned it from and those that benefit from it; the athlete's fidelity to their sport binds them to their trainers and fellow competitors; the researcher's fidelity to scientific methods binds them to their research community (for all that the empirical sciences sometimes foster a perverse obfuscation of their human dimension); the artist's fidelity to their craft binds them not only to the lineages of art that inspire them, but to communities of appreciators without whom their work is incomplete. Fidelity, therefore, is the root of knowledge and also the wellspring of community and culture. To lack fidelity is to become, as traced at the beginning of this discussion, a cultural nomad, and this is not freedom but a kind of ephemeral prison, where we exchange our individuality for convenience.

As cyborgs, we are assaulted by habit-forming situations because commercial technology is designed, from the ground upwards, to be addictive, to form habits that turn to desire rather than fidelity, to addiction rather than knowledge. Take, as the smallest example, your relationship with your smartphone. By design, this robot is not intended to last, it is not meant for repair beyond trivial interventions (a broken screen, for instance). It is intended to habituate you to its action before being rendered obsolete by the escalating scales of computing power that drive hardware sales. The announcement of a new iPhone or Android phone is intended to push our buttons and draw us into 'upgrading', a euphemism that politely disguises what it really means: indulging an addiction to the new. This critique can be challenged, of course, but to argue that 'upgrading' increases utility is to fall prey to the moral disaster of consequentialism – and thus be shallow-sighted.

Although I am no fan of motor vehicles, I would like to compare the way cars were designed fifty years ago to the way they are designed now. For it is not a coincidence that classic cars are still in service: they were built to last, and designed for repair. A mechanic of my father's generation could show fidelity towards the design and function of the engines and mechanisms of cars at that time and thus gain knowledge of them. Today, the core function of an automobile is barred to all but the sorcerers of manufacturing, and an onboard robot controls almost all functions, thus reducing the work of a mechanic to merely substituting faulty components when instructed. These are machines built for obsolescence that bar all practical knowledge of their workings except as proprietary trade secrets. In short, the design of contemporary high-tech machines aims at dependence, and this cyber-dependence is the first principle of commercial technology. It is not a coincidence that the clockwork torch (or flashlight) was designed for Africa, a less commercial market, and not the 'developed' world. 'Developed' here is a synonym for 'dependent'.

Thus Facebook (or any other social media platform for that matter) is designed not for fidelity, nor for binding people together in practices that foster knowledge, but for dependence and addiction. Follows and shares are the motivating force by design, and this pursuit of metrics to measure 'social success' serves to substitute dependence for fidelity and addiction for community. That is not to say that fidelity to friendship cannot be expressed through these purportedly conversational media – merely that they are not *designed* to support it. They are created for cyber-dependence, and the utility of the communicative networks they create blinds us to this in yet another example of shallow-sightedness. It is scarcely surprising that propaganda, or 'fake news', as it has been recently dubbed, thrives in systems that discourage fidelity and thus minimise productive community. Knowledge requires fidelity to a practice; when it is reduced to merely repeating what we have heard, we come adrift from our epistemic moorings, as Wikipedia, that methodical aggregator of the trivia of corporate-owned media, epitomises.

What would cyber-fidelity mean, and could we imagine technology built for it? Fidelity is founded on the promise (literal or figurative) to be part of something and thus to foster knowledge within that community (whether we are talking sports, research, art, crafts, or anything else). Cyber-fidelity would therefore apply whenever our robots aided our commitment and our communities without simultaneously engendering our dependency. At the moment, whatever fidelity is expressed via the internet does so *against* the prevailing winds of dependency. If you wish to learn about fidelity, you will find exemplars more easily in the so-called Third World than in the Dependent World we live in. Hence the suggestion that there is a pressing need to technologise the planet is another aspect of the moral disaster of consequentialism. The free 'Third' world does not need to learn our dependencies from us. Colonial occupation already established dependencies that will not be resolved by adding technological addiction to economies that were optimised for colonial export and that always acted as cyber-dependencies, long before computers upped the ante.

What I am calling cyber-fidelity is another name for what Ivan Illich called *convivial tools*; technology that empowers individuals within their communities, rather than creating dependence and dividing or destroying community in the name of 'progress' (the consequentialist war-cry par excellence). The bicycle versus the car is just one example of cyber-fidelity versus cyber-dependence — and here it is not a mere footnote that the former fosters physical fitness and mechanical skill through maintenance, while the latter fosters 'road rage' and planned obsolescence. Note that both cars and bicycles are products of overlapping technological networks: tyres, gears, steering... however, one empowers its human and community, and the other fosters dependencies on manufacturing, oil, and infrastructures that are far from egalitarian.

When I asked earlier if dogs could express fidelity, what was at stake was a distinction between habit and dependence, and now I can suggest another aspect of this question: the dog's commitment to its pack is the evidence of its fidelity. The dog not only belongs to a community – and for domestic dogs, that means both the humans they live with and the neighbourhood dogs they fraternise with – but it has knowledge of that community. Indeed, it is the principal knowledge that any dog learns. The dog cares which other dogs have been in the park recently, and cannot wait to be reunited with members of its pack as they come back home. The dog, in other words, is a convivial *being*, as (in its own way) is the cat. The human too has this capacity; we are, as Donna Haraway suggested, a companion species to our dogs and cats, and rather less so in the context of our robots.

Like cars, computers opened up a space that could be convivial or could fall into dependency – and at this point it seems clear which way they have gone. Nothing marks me out as a heretic in our cyber-dependant society quite as spectacularly as my suggestion that we have more to learn from the traditional cultures of the Third World than they can benefit from moving uncritically towards the Dependent World we live in. If we wish to build computers that can foster cyber-fidelity, perhaps we should look to the clockwork torch and the way it was designed to be of use *outside* our enmeshing networks of technology. I do not know what a convivial computer might be; I do not know whether cyber-fidelity is even possible in a world of robots – but we have truly narrowed our horizons of possibility to mere technological addiction if we cannot even imagine trying to explore this uncharted and unimagined frontier.

VI. FALLEN VIRTUE

The last three virtues I want to consider are courage,
justice, and honesty. These are all qualities that Alasdair
MacIntyre — who has perhaps done more than anyone in the last
century to revive interest in virtues — suggests are essential to any
successful practice. If so, then the cybervirtues of cyber-courage,
cyber-justice, and cyber-honesty would be especially vital, given the
discussion in the previous chapter concerning the importance of fidelity
for sustaining practices. However, when we look at our relationship
with technology, we are far more likely to find the cyber-debilities of
cyber-cowardice, cyber-indignance, and cyber-deceit. Perhaps
precisely because of the problems with fidelity, the virtues
that sustain practices are those most threatened by
contemporary technology.

Technological Cowardice

In the heroic age of ancient Greece, the Norse Vikings and
Celtic warriors, courage was the central virtue around which
society revolved. This was not just in battle but everywhere in
life: to lack the courage to do what was required of you was
to bring shame upon yourself and your kin. Fidelity was an
important part of this, and Alasdair MacIntyre suggests this
was the primary virtue expected of women during this time,
but that is not to say it affected women *only*; indeed, in feudal
China, fidelity was arguably more central to a virtuous man
than courage. To be alive in the heroic age was to be bound
to blood relatives that you were expected to defend in both
body and honour — even if, in so doing, you would meet your
death. To die was everyone's fate, and this awareness — which

we have lost sight of today – provided the backdrop against which courage gained its meaning.

Today, we are inclined to view such situations negatively, emphasising not the culture of valour that mattered to the people of that time, but the ways these stifling strictures of honour suppressed individual liberty and freedom. There is an element of truth to this criticism, yet there is a danger too, one entangled with the moral disaster of individualism and brought into focus by the problems with fidelity discussed in the previous chapter. For without a common bond against which the exercise of courage acquires its meaning, we either lose sight of what courage is, or mistakenly identify valour only with outraged dignity – indignance is *not* courage, and I will come back to this later on. The ease with which our digital public spaces permit us to scratch this itch only deepens the crisis. How do we know if we are brave, when all measure of courage has been lost to us?

A robot cannot show cyber-courage in any individual manner, for it fears nothing and is thus incapable of valour as we understand it. This very absence of both fearfulness *and* courageousness is precisely why robots are such appealing 'soldiers' when war is conditioned solely by the moral disaster of consequentialism, as it became in the great wars of the twentieth century and never ceased being since. But before we consider the abject failure of these conflicts we ought to consider whether cyber-courage is even a plausible concept – for the evidence of the effects of technology upon this virtue is primarily of the exact opposite.

For MacIntyre, courage was not only the primary virtue of the heroic age, but a central virtue in any situation. Virtues are qualities that acquire their meaning from the practices that people pursue together, since only in a shared context do qualitative judgements possess a common ground. MacIntyre suggests three cornerstone virtues are indispensable to any tradition, since without them even maintaining a practice becomes implausible. Truthfulness and a sense of justice are the two virtues required to maintain a viable community, while courage is required to do the right thing, even when it is difficult. Indeed, the most basic understanding of courageousness is as the capacity to act when others would not, and this is vanishingly far from the mere willingness to display outrage, which need not be virtuous.

For a cyborg to display cyber-courage, a robot would need to be capable of encouraging its human to assert themselves virtuously: but how would it know? Precisely the failure of Artificial Intelligence has been the discovery, slow to be accepted, that computational intelligence is divorced from the practices of beings. All animals understand their situation through being able to coordinate their memories and habits within their own imagination, which 'fills in the blanks' of every circumstance through means so familiar to us that we take it for granted. Yet no robot can do this. The computational efficiency of silicon chips creates an impression of greater mental power because complex calculations are hard for us yet easy for robots. But calculation is a very small aspect of our cognitive capabilities – and for computers, it is all they have. To exist as a being is to live within a world, and this capacity is something no robots currently possesses, nor is it likely that they will on the current design principles for software.

Rather than cyber-courage, what we have seen with the growing presence of computers in all aspects of human life is an erosion of courage as robots become the point of confrontation, and humans are able to distance themselves from their actions. The internet troll – the twenty-first century's resident schoolyard bully – is emboldened to make verbal attacks on strangers precisely because it is only a computer that is in personal contact with their victim. Bullying had long been associated with cowardice, its psychological appeal resting on the illusion of power created by picking on those who seem powerless to stop you. In the playground or workplace, the bully chooses to target only those who can be successfully intimidated. The cyber-cowardice engendered by our digital public spaces so successfully isolates trolls from their actions, the risk of reprisal falls to almost nothing. The virtual mask stokes the confidence of trolls, but courage is more than just asserting your indignation; there is nothing courageous about skulking in the shadows and preying upon others who have no capacity for reprisal or restitution.

In the heroic age, the fundamental display of courage was upon the battlefield. There, warriors braved death to defend their brothers in arms, and their families and clans for whom defeat could mean slavery, rape, or death. There is still courage to be found among today's soldiers, but it is threatened by the cyber-cowardice that offers the capacity to kill without any risk of injury in return. Armed drones, a grotesque modification of equipment originally intended merely for surveillance, allow missile strikes on distant lands without any risk of personal harm to the operator. Here is the ultimate example of cyber-cowardice, a technology that extinguishes the flame of valour that burns in all those who serve in armed forces and dishonours entire nations such as the United Kingdom and the United States who have turned to these robotic weapons as a means of assassination.

Bradley Strawser is the ethicist who has made the strongest case for the moral permissibility of drones. He points to the psychological stress upon drone pilots, and the terrible post-traumatic stress caused by watching people die on a screen. He suggests it takes intellectual bravery and moral courage to fly drones... but is this not the cyber-cowardice of the internet troll elevated to its most extreme degree? Laurie Calhoun draws exactly the opposite conclusion from the psychological impact of being a killer drone pilot: it demonstrates that they *do* feel remorse for taking the lives of their victims. Perhaps the most that can be said in defence of the armed drone pilot is that unlike the troll, they suffer for what they do.

I have respect for Strawser, who has engaged with the moral problems of armed drones in a way that is honourable, for all that I radically disagree with his conclusions. He has suggested that the perceived problems with armed drones spring from the intuitive asymmetry of the battlefield where one side can kill without risk. His claim is that this imbalance was already present when jet fighters faced off against guerrillas armed with shoulder-mounted missiles, who could not be deemed remotely equivalent in power. Yet the fighter pilot still put themselves at risk in this scenario: there is not just a difference of degree involved in the use of armed drones, the ratio of risk between combatants has become *infinite* – courage cannot survive this asymptotic chasm, and the psychological cost of being part of an armed drone cyborg is evidence of the depravity of this technology, not of any form of courage.

What makes the armed drone seem acceptable is the moral disaster of consequentialism, which sees morality as reducible to calculation. Thus Strawser's view is that the capacity to complete a mission without risking a soldier is morally obligatory – provided, he repeatedly stresses, that the cause is just. But good ends cannot justify despicable means, and the battlefield emptied of valour ceases to be a site of anything honourable. Indeed, it is no longer a battlefield, but merely the place where extermination takes place in pursuit of a victory that gets further from reach when such robotic weapons are deployed. Every civilian killed or injured in a drone strike sees nothing but the horror of death brought about by a cyborg enemy too cowardly even to show its face.

Everybody's Got Justice Wrong Except You

The problems with technological cowardice are a sign that something has gone horribly wrong, and the root problem in this regard is that justice is something nearly everyone cares about, but everybody has a different sense of what it is. The virtue of cyber-justice is one that is, therefore, near-impossible to imagine, because justice itself has become morally ambiguous. This problem, upon which ethics has flailed since at least Nietzsche, divides moral philosophers into those who assert there is a perfect rational standard of justice, and those that claim there never could be such a thing. This conflict is not worth buying into on either side. What matters instead is the recognition that there *are* a set of ideals for justice, as well as for related concepts such as fairness and 'just war', and that these ideals will only possess a rational standard if they are shared. When no such practice of shared ideals exists, chaos reigns, as nobody is agreed upon what to aim for, and mutual trust is impossible. I am appreciative of this chaotic supernova of individual freedom, even while I am a critic of its underlying lack of fidelity and see it as exacerbating already severe problems. For if there is no path towards any common sense of justice, injustice proliferates and escalates in its absence.

Before considering what it would mean for a robot and its human to be just, we must consider the debilities and defects that result from the chaos nova around us, amply embodied in gigacyberg digital public spaces such as Twitter and Facebook. It is by seeing how things go wrong that we can discover ways to rescue justice, and thus propose a virtue of justice for cyborgs.

One defect is quick to discuss: *nihilism*, the self-defeating faith in there being nothing worth having faith in. Nihilism is borne of a rigid conviction in the value of truth (such as the Abrahamic traditions bequeathed to the sciences) coming up against the unjustifiable circumstances of that conviction. Here is where a person from a faith tradition like Christianity or Islam or some of the Hindu practices makes a leap of faith. The nihilist makes a similar leap into believing nothing has value – without noticing the unwavering faith in standards of judgement required to get to such an absurd position. Thus, the nihilist is confused into justifying anything on grounds of nothing. There's not much we can do to help such unfortunate cynics: like viruses that infect humans and robots, you just have to put up with the trouble they cause, and defend against them as best you can.

Holding ideals of justice so strongly that faith passes into the condition of certainty describes the debility I shall call *indignance* – which becomes evident whenever someone displays their indignation rather too freely. Here, as with the certainty of blind faith in religion or nationalism, people *know* they are right. This empowers them to act in all manner of atrocious ways – particularly when they are acting as internet cyborgs. Sometimes, this *cyber-indignance* manifests as a desire to dole out punishment, a kind of 'digital vigilantism'. Fuelled by the cyber-cruelty invoked by loners in masks, such self-righteous cyborgs sometimes deploy despicable methods in the name of their own kind of rough justice, such as 'doxxing' (releasing personal data, such as a home address) or death threats. Here, the underlying indignant certainty has deceived the cyborgs in question into thinking their methods are not important – their moral certainty, ironically, makes them behave as nihilists, turning to terror as a weapon as if nothing mattered but being on the right side of an argument. They have an unfortunate role model in this: both megacyborg nations and their guerrilla enemies have been employing terror and death as ill-considered weapons for decades.

More often, however, cyber-indignance is all bark and little bite. Passing angry judgements on what you find vile and disgusting is fairly typical human behaviour (as is acting out behind a mask, for that matter), but tirades of cyber-disdain do nothing but antagonise those being judged or encourage others to hurl further abuse. There is no persuasive force to this form of argument: you instantly drive a wedge between yourself and whomsoever is being reviled, and, as with the resort to terror as a weapon, it rests on the certainty that others must be wrong. In these kinds of situations, however, this is at least restrained by an acute sense that there should be limits to which methods are permitted, and this is the principal redeeming quality to this kind of preachy outburst.

Those that do not lose sight of the importance of *methods* recognise that some courses of action could never be just, and should not be pursued. To think otherwise is to fall into the moral disaster of consequentialism, to think only outcomes matter because of the understandable emphasis we place on how things turn out. But considering the choice of method is part of how anyone ensures their desired long-term outcome. In fact, exactly what makes certain methods *unjust* is their exclusion from any viable idea of 'justice' that is not merely revenge dressed up in convenient justifications. Nothing is worth achieving 'at any cost', although there are things that ought to be defended with every just method available. Thinking otherwise is to fail at being a just cyborg of any kind, because all extreme methods make justice harder – even impossible – to attain, and thus entail an element of self-defeat. Any kind of digital vigilantism that turns to doxxing, trolling or death threats has lost sight of justice.

Justice is fragile, a sliding puzzle that can be aligned but never completed – a Rubik's Cube with the wrong number of pieces in each colour. The judicial system itself is an acknowledgment of this: it's not enough to administer a rigid system of rules, as judges are charged with doing. There are times where an uncertain moral judgement must be made in order to render a legal judgement, which is precisely what a jury can provide. In both justice and morality, reliable judgement is all but impossible to attain as individuals, since it is only when a particular set of ideals are weighed in a specific context that an answer to a moral question can be produced. This requires a common moral practice, and this depends on prior experience and the skill this develops. An individual can make judgements about others, but not reliably without the counsel of others, and in considering their own behaviour an individual is all too often an unreliable judge.

Can cyborgs be *cyber-just*? It is difficult for this to happen, because robots do not live in a world, and thus justice is as alien to them as bravery. However, a robot can still behave in cyber-just, cyber-indignant, or cyber-nihilist ways towards humans as a consequence of its design. Computer viruses are a perfect example of cyber-nihilism, since they act against the humans they encounter as a result of the absence of moral judgement entailed in their creation. Online discussion media that carelessly censor curse words can act with cyber-indignance, for example when they censor words like 'Dickensian' because they contain a swear word. It is less easy to imagine an instance of a robot being cyber-just towards its human, although it could be argued that passwords and biometric security are cyber-just, in that they uphold property law and personal privacy with the unquenchable zeal of a machine.

The social sense of cyber-justice – encouraging a cyborg to act with a clear sense of justice – is a case where there may yet be possibilities. Key to ethical knowledge is *moral representation*, the sharing and discussing of quandaries and dilemmas. This happens temporarily in a jury room, intermittently in a confessional booth, and also quite often in a pub. Whether it's between priest and parishioner or a couple of friends, ethical thought requires a shared perspective. Moral representation is in no way exclusive to religion, although it is inherent to authentic religious practice to engage in some kind of moral representation, and when this is absent – particularly when demagogues stir up one-sided indignation – the result is an ethical failure.

To form a moral practice requires discourse to offset the inherent fragility of justice, which is never wholly reducible to rule-following, as Alasdair MacIntyre cautions. Even Kant, who is most associated with rule-focused ethics, recognised this, and thus held that virtue and self-improvement were central to an ethical life (in contrast to how his views are usually presented). Besides, as Wittgenstein made clear, rule-following itself is a practice for beings such as humans. We are not robots who can exercise instructions unthinkingly: there is always a background of understanding that gives a set of rules its distinctive context – and in the absence of this subtle understanding, a 'thing' lacks what is required to understand justice.

Designing a robot to facilitate cyber-just cyborgs might yet be possible by allowing for moral representation. We could leverage the network properties of digital public spaces to help people make moral judgements, and to defer the cyber-indignance inflamed by the culture clash of the internet. In some respects, this is already happening wherever humans discuss ethical problems online, but it could be enhanced by the design of mechanisms to foster discourse of the relevant kind. Sometimes, this will occur in private between individuals, as in the confessional or the bar booth, sometimes in closed groups like the jury room, perhaps it could even happen in public if indignation could be appropriately constrained. All that is required to head in a more helpful direction is to get beyond thinking that everyone has it wrong except you and those who happen to agree with you. This blight of certainty has become the greatest threat to moral practices of all kinds, for ethical knowledge is neither scientific nor calculable, but always entails the doubt that comes from knowing that you might be wrong.

Is The Truth Still Out There?
Courage and justice are two of MacIntyre's cornerstone virtues, without which no practice can maintain its community. The final virtue he highlights in this regard is truthfulness, but, like justice, this is a difficult concept for us to bring to bear against the background of the chaos nova. Precisely the problem that has shattered consensus is the widespread disagreement about truth, which raises the awkward question of whether it is possible to be truthful without understanding the truth. When our sense of truth vanishes, what does it mean to be honest?

At a time when 'fake news' and 'alternative facts' have become everyday points of discussion, it may indeed seem we have lost our moorings with respect to the truth. This growing crisis of knowledge has been long recognised by philosophers, and indeed many other academics, and what we are seeing now is less the breakdown of the truth than it is the dawning public realisation of the extent of a problem that had previously been corralled within the ivory towers. Part of the problem we are facing is that understanding knowledge in terms of what *is* or *is not* true makes it seem as if knowing is just a matter of having the correct set of statements. The situation seems very different when the facts are understood as something created through the exercise of the practices of authentic knowledge.

You have knowledge whenever you are able to act reliably. For example, you have practical knowledge of a car when you can repair it reliably; you have social knowledge of people when you can communicate reliably with them; you have scientific knowledge of an alpha particle when you can detect it reliably. Telling another person how a car works, or where people go, or what an alpha particle is doesn't necessarily show knowledge. It is often just repeating what you have heard from those with authentic knowledge. The facts are true when the practices from which they emerge are reliable.

When we are not the person with the knowledge, what matters is whether we are being a *reliable witness* to those that do. This idea, drawn out in a novel way by chemist-turned-philosopher Isabelle Stengers, connects all situations where facts are being claimed. For Stengers, when a researcher acquires knowledge of an alpha particle, they are a reliable witness *for the alpha particle*, making a great deal of scientific research into finding ways to make inanimate objects 'speak'. To have the facts is to be connected to the knowledge that established them by a chain of reliable witnesses, where you are the final link in the chain. On this understanding, the truth of the facts is peripheral to there being both an authentic knowledge at the root of any claim, and a chain of reliable witnesses from this to whomever is speaking.

When we take 'being truthful' to be about stating true facts, it can obscure the moral qualities relevant to the virtue of *honesty*. There is something to be said for the Christian phrasing 'bearing false witness' as a way of expressing the debility of deceitfulness: this description stresses the breaking of the chain of reliable witnesses, and makes the standard of virtue hinge upon the act of *witnessing for others* rather than *having the true facts* – as if human honesty were a surrogate for forensic investigation or empirical experiments. To be honest or sincere is to be a reliable witness, whenever that is what is called for. When someone has a terrible haircut, for instance, remarking on how striking it looks is a very different response from telling them they should always use that hairdresser! Withholding comment is not necessarily a sign of dishonesty, and other virtues such as tact may make remaining silent or being selective with remarks appropriate choices in many situations. Only when we explicitly bear false witness have we acted with tangible deceitfulness.

As cyborgs, however, we are constantly tempted into bearing false witness. When a story comes to us through the digital public spaces, we sometimes retweet, reshare, or otherwise propagate unreliable witnesses – our sharing of these stories is acting as a witness, and as such there is a tacit duty to at least minimally confirm the veracity of what we are passing down the chain. Our robots are, in these cases, incapable of being cyber-deceitful: they reliably repeat what was said. Yet at the same time, cyborgs communicating in this way are *cyber-gullible*: the sheer ease with which whatever attracts our attention gets flagged for repeating discourages careful checking of what is being claimed – especially when the political and ideological leanings of the message align with the human's view of the world. Thus 'fake news', which is the propagation of false witness, can proliferate easily.

Could we design digital public spaces to be *cyber-honest* instead? Even the decision to work towards this would be a severe break from the tenor of the internet, where click-bait is carefully cultivated to misrepresent or to package vacuous fluff as if it were interesting, all in the relentless pursuit of our attention. Yet it does not seem inherently impossible to design for cyber-honesty, although any mechanism for drawing attention to the implausibility of possibly-fake online claims runs the risk of being abused – it might exacerbate cyber-bluntness, perhaps to the point of cruelty. A system for flagging errors or deceit would risk producing all the same problems as public karma systems that track negative behaviour – the potential for abuse could make anything like this untenable, unless there was a high cost to blowing the whistle.

One possibility worth considering is a 'warning flag' that could be used to challenge a story as deceitful. To prevent abuse, these flags might have to be kept hidden from public eyes until a sufficient number had been raised, or until at least one flag had been raised by someone who had earned a trustworthy status in such matters. Trust in such a system could be staked: raising your flag unduly might result in the availability of that flag being withdrawn for a progressive period of time afterwards. In such an arrangement, deploying a flag frivolously would be to lose it for a while, whilst a vindicated objection would raise trust ratings and perhaps provide additional flags. This system, if it could be made to work, would offer cyborgs the chance to become akin to honesty sheriffs on the digital frontier (at least for those willing to put in the time required to check the veracity of claims) while most would be free to ignore flagging procedures yet still be informed when a duplicitous story was being shared. It perhaps would be best if no story was ever *prevented* from being shared, and if flag-raising only affected the trust rating of that individual story, since the alternative would be censorship.

Such a system requires moderators at first, but as cyborgs earn trust within the system they could eventually operate without direct oversight, helping to overcome the scale problem that afflicts networks like Twitter and Facebook. In some respects, this proposal is not dissimilar to the way spam reporting works in certain contexts. The blogging platform Typepad, for instance, allows blog owners to manually flag spam comments, immediately deleting them and then watching for the same messages elsewhere in the blogs they manage. Such an approach would not work in the larger digital public spaces precisely because of the collective qualities of these networks, but with a blog (where ownership is clear) they are adequate to the task they were designed for. It's not clear whether anyone has thought about expanding these kind of nuisance defences to 'fake news', but this is something worth exploring now that the cyber-deceitfulness of 'social' media has become a significant problem.

An objection may occur: how to deal with messages like a Christian posting 'Jesus is the saviour of the world', or a Discordian posting 'Did you know God's name is Eris and that he is a girl?' If we think in terms of the truth of a statement, flags might be raised. But these cases entail no false witness, any more than do claims like 'The USA is the greatest nation on Earth' or 'The US is the greatest threat to the planet'. It is not because these are 'just opinions' that they are not examples of deceit, but because they are sincerely-made statements entailing no claim to knowledge (understood as guiding reliable actions). Faith traditions do entail knowledge (of rituals, hymns, community life and so forth), but never *metaphysical* knowledge, as such – if they did, there would be no question of faith in connection with them, and unwavering blind faith is always bad faith.

Stemming the growing tide of cyber-deceit – the use of the internet as a self-selecting propaganda machine – will entail taking a stand on knowledge. This may involve improving our collective critical skills, or at least taking a greater care to distinguish deceitful statements from sincere but untestable, accidentally mistaken, or reliably grounded ones. False witness depends upon someone *falsifying* a claim or repeating a falsified claim carelessly; these are not the same as bearing witness in a situation where no viable knowledge can be claimed, and we need to be clear about how we know things to understand the boundaries.

Note that sharing the claims of someone who disagrees with 'scientific consensus' is *not* bearing false witness, no matter how much we disagree with what is said. Viewing knowledge as a bag of true statements deceives us in this regard, and we need to become smarter about tolerating *dissensus,* Jacques Rancière's concept which acknowledges that politics requires the recognition of disagreement, or else it cannot be a space for discussing how to live together but only an empty power struggle to enforce a pre-conceived consensus. As Rancière warns, democracy is impossible without disagreement. The key problem here is deceit, which is always a moral weakness even when applied in pursuit of a supposed greater good. The unintentional false witness of our digital public spaces is merely the amplifier that transforms 'fake news' from problem to crisis.

Deceit goes beyond the tactful presentation of your views – there are always infinite ways to present your perspective, after all, and bluntness should not be unduly conflated with honesty. Deceit is the intent to deny respect by purposefully bearing false witness. We have let ourselves become so accustomed to duplicity that we think there is nothing we can do about it. We can still change this, but only if we discern treacherous speech from its alternatives. The truth was never out there – reality is out there, and that was never true but merely, unwaveringly *there*. The truth is what is sometimes revealed by authentic knowledge, and what is always destroyed by false witness. If we aim to be reliable witnesses, and place our trust in those who know how to repeat honestly, sincerely, and, indeed, truthfully, we can get far closer to the truth than we have so far managed.

VII. BECOMING GOOD CYBORGS

What is the good life for a cyborg? This question is the elusive grail that I have sought by writing this book. The nine virtues and cybervirtues that I have explored in the preceding chapters are not intended to be a complete set, but rather are signposts that mark out the territory we are currently lost within. By considering the problems of technology – the debilities afflicting us as cyborgs – and also by reflecting upon those situations where virtue has survived a collision with high technology, I hope to have offered a navigational chart for the ethical landscape we are living within. But as with all treasure maps, it needs decoding – and we may find that seeking the prize is not as important as having looked for it at all.

Fidelity: faithfulness to a practice, institution, ideal, or person, is the foundational virtue for the cyborg good life as I have sketched it. Without a tether to some kind of worthwhile practice we are merely cultural nomads and the commercial cyberg and its progeny will simply distract us within their radical monopolies. We need a better perspective on the good than the ones that are sold to us. There is, thankfully, more fidelity in our world than it might at first seem. Musicians and artists have fidelity to the practices that make their artworks worthwhile, and I am heartened to find this also happening in games as they mature as an artistic medium. Researchers have fidelity to the ideals of the sciences and to their unique practices of investigation. Teachers possess a faithfulness towards their students whenever they are not dragged down by the prescriptive pressures of an imposed curriculum or commercial anxieties.

Unlike many contemporary thinkers, I am not unduly pessimistic about fidelity towards religious traditions either. The problems associated with this sphere of life are mirrored in nationalistic traditions that seem far more troublesome, and in many cases distinguishing between 'religion' and 'nation' as a root cause of some conflict is utterly futile. Fidelity to a community of religious practice is something that I admire, in part perhaps because I have been trapped between different spiritual traditions for some time now and lack a shared community. But at the same time, I see a great deal of bad faith in religious and non-religious practice today – excessive certainty, and betrayal of the ideals at the core of authentic spiritual paths. I just don't see the category of 'religion' as having any especial role in these specific kinds of problem.

I ended the discussion of virtues by focusing upon the three that Alasdair MacIntyre considered central to any tradition – courage, a sense of justice, and truthfulness. MacIntyre famously converted to Catholicism because it was the tradition he felt most able to express fidelity towards, and his perspective on virtue is undeniably Christian, even though he expertly takes into account the historical background of virtue from the ancient Greeks onwards. I concur with his sense of the central role these three virtues play in sustaining practices and traditions. Courage is required to do what one knows is right, and knowledge of the right path requires a sense of justice and the honesty to speak truth, even and especially to those in power. However, these three virtues are placed under intolerable strain as a result of our technology and the mindset that accompanies it.

You may not share my concern about armed drones extinguishing courage as it once existed on the battlefield, but the complete collapse of faith in what is *true* is something that should trouble us all. We cannot hope to find anything like 'the good life' without securing at least some viable way of understanding truth. The concept of 'reliable witness' that I have taken from Isabelle Stengers and developed into my own concept of knowledge-as-practice strikes me as an essential corrective to merely shrugging and rejecting that there is any such thing as 'truth' – as I once did myself. The possibility of different practices giving varying perspectives on what is true does not undermine anything but the most simplistic concepts of truth. What is *true* is the sum of everything that can be reliably witnessed: that these diverse accounts require reconciling is not at all the same as saying nothing is true.

Part of the reason that I consider fidelity foundational to the cyborg good life is that the problems of justice – which are intimately related to the problems with truth – can only be addressed by ensuring adequate moral representation. This requires fidelity, at the very least towards individuals, but also to traditions or practices that provide a common community in which the sharing of ethical concerns and problems can take place. Friends, family, lovers, husbands, wives... there is no 'good life' when you are alone, and there is no way for justice to regain its footing without recognising the need for moral representation. The twin moral disasters that have eroded fidelity also undermine justice either by misrepresenting the freedom of the individual (and thus degrading community): the disaster of *individualism*, or by seeming to offer a shortcut such that what is right can be calculated: the disaster of *consequentialism*. The good life does not emerge from an algorithm.

I purposefully began the discussion of virtue with an Eastern philosophical tradition, to provide some counterpoint to ending with the Christian perspective of MacIntyre. Like Heidegger, I find much of value in the spiritual and ethical traditions of India, China, and their neighbours. However, the problems of technology have not been escaped by those who live among the rivers that flow from the Himalayas. In the wisdom of the Taoist sages, I find the inspiration to maintain restraint against the temptations the commercial cybergs constantly buffet us with. The cyborg 'good life' may well be simpler than the one we have – although what 'simple' means to a cyborg might require some thought.

Another advantage of turning to Taoist thought is that the humility of this tradition has something more to offer beyond the Enlightenment virtue of respect, which I compared it to. All things are equal with respect to the Tao, the sages say. And, while the equality of humanity that Kant and others developed out of Christian philosophical roots means a great deal to me, we also need to find ways to extend respect to non-humans, both living and otherwise. A cyborg 'good life' that was not sustainable would be a sham, and finding a way to avoid that mistake requires a respect for our planet that is utterly threatened by the moral disaster of consequentialism.

The Abrahamic traditions – and, indeed, many of the traditions that grow out of Judaism, Christianity, and Islam, such as the contemporary sciences – all knowingly or unknowingly assign a special place for the human (as, for instance, the animal capable of conducting research). I personally do not think this is misguided, since our immense capacity for imagination places us in an extremely unique relationship with all things. However, it is a betrayal towards any and all humanistic traditions if it is not understood that stewardship of our planet is part of the deal. It really doesn't matter if you want to put this in terms of God assigning the duty of care for the living world or in terms of the rationality of not destroying the conditions for our species' continuing existence. From a certain vantage point, these claims are entirely the same.

Once we recognise that human equality does not pre-clude the deeper equalities that the Taoist sages gesture at, we are in a position to appreciate that respect and kindness does not end at our species. Tremendous violence is done to the earth in order to bring us our robots: something is seri-ously wrong, therefore, when we treat out smartphones and computers as commodities to use up and discard. Even a ro-bot deserves our respect. This does not necessarily mean that we should act kindly towards an iPhone, although there may well be merit in doing so. It only means that there is nothing virtuous in intentional waste, and nothing good in planned obsolescence.

Ivan Illich warned that 'the better is the enemy of the good', an old proverb sometimes attributed to Voltaire. The point is that constantly looking for 'better' technology makes working out what *good* technology might look like im-possible... The goals are constantly shifting, and we seldom have time to work out what's going on before what we were figuring out has already been replaced by something new. As Heidegger tried to make clear, the mindset of technology that makes everything into 'standing reserve' – something for us to use – distorts our understanding of our tools. This is the moral disaster of consequentialism in its guise of utility: everything is there to be *used* – even us. Einstein summed this up beau-tifully when he suggested that our time is characterised by a perfection of means accompanied by confusion about goals.

Each of the discussions of cybervirtue within this book shows how ignoring our tools, treating them as morally and practically neutral, entails a serious failure of thought. As cyborgs, we are substantially affected by the robots we have made essential to our being, and those robots are substantially affected by the cybergs that built and maintain them. If it seems impossible that we can affect the corporate manufacture of commercial commodities, it is only because we are daunted by the scale of our cybernetic networks whenever we are able to notice them. As humans, we have more power to influence the world we live in than anything else that draws breath. Why do we doubt that we can change the world — *when we already have?*

However, for the cyborg 'good life' to be more than a wishful ideal, we need to move beyond defensively fortifying our conceptual borders. We cannot afford to be entirely trapped inside those practices and traditions to which we remain faithful. Not everyone can become a traveller in an ethical multiverse, as I unwittingly discovered I have become. Not everyone is able to live alongside the many different moral worlds that collide in the chaos nova. Most people require a grounded sense of their world, and that focuses them towards a single perspective. The 'good life' might well require a grounded sense of the world, but this possibility is threatened when one person's perspective collides with other ways of being, creating aggressive conflicts.

The conditions of existence at this time mean that humanity cannot be united into any single world of experience, which means that the cyborg 'good life' is always more than one thing. Fidelity towards many different practices is the unavoidable circumstance of our collective being. This makes tact an extremely important virtue to develop, and cyber-tact something that we ought to find ways to develop. We have to be able to recognise other ways of being, even those that we might have difficulty appreciating, and this cannot happen simply by launching into a crusade for some pre-set image of justice. Constructing a way of living *together* will mean having to talk to each other, with tact and understanding.

Finally, there is that personal virtue that perhaps feels closest in tone to fidelity, tenacity. If *fidelity* is what binds us to other humans and their shared practices, *tenacity* is what gives us the capacity to push forward on a difficult path, whether alone or together. To develop the 'good life' for ourselves as cyborgs, we're going to need more than fidelity to our practices. We are going to need to envisage how to make *good* robots (rather than always-better ones), and we're going to have to solve the difficulties involved in designing for cybervirtue, as well as the problems entailed in exercising it. This requires both the vision to imagine what is needed, and the tenacity to persevere towards making it happen. Perhaps this is a challenge that our robots might be able to help us with.

CODA/OVERTURE

So, who is the virtuous cyborg? It is the human robot pairing that is able to manifest at least *some* virtues; an ideal entity, in the sense that it is imagined, but a very real possibility all the same. A robot which was designed to express cybervirtues would make the virtuous cyborg something easier for a greater number of humans to aspire to, and it is this possibility that I am trying to highlight with this book. While we are enmeshed within cybergs that are corrupted by the twin moral disasters of our time (individualism and consequentialism), it is far harder for any of us to embody the figure of the virtuous cyborg, and this is a far bigger problem than it may at first appear.

Must we, then, give up our smartphones and our laptops? It is not even worth making this suggestion, for we shall not do so, and this is, of course, part of the essential crisis we are facing. Indeed, it would be far easier to dismiss the concept of 'virtue' as anything relevant to ethical life than to consider this absurd suggestion – and no doubt some people who encounter this book will do so. But equally, I hope at least some of my discussions of virtue within this book make it clear that living a 'good life' means possessing at least *some* virtues, and in this respect, denying virtue as a concept means to give up any chance of a good life. I am not arguing that virtue ethics is the only way of thinking about morals: it isn't. It's not even my favourite of the choices available. But when all of our ethical thought has been corrupted, virtue seems like the most viable place to attempt a rescue.

This is the coda to *The Virtuous Cyborg*, but it is also the overture to what must happen next: a conversation – a great many conversations, really – about the virtues of humans, the cybervirtues of our robot-human pairings, and our understanding of knowledge. Our attempts at making things better have brought us to the brink of disaster, and if the situation is not quite as bad as it seems, it is still probably worse than we are willing to admit. I love humans, I love our hopelessly flawed robots, I love the plants that support us and our animal companions that live and die with us, and I love our glorious green-blue planet – I even love, in some perverse way, the mess we have made of everything. Let's not do better... Let us discover instead what might be good.

GLOSSARY

Actor-network theory: a framework for understanding the interaction between *beings* and *things,* such that both possess *agency* (q.q.v.). While decisions are made by beings, the decisions made are affected by the qualities of things, so both are considered actors within a network of other actors.

Age of Distraction: my preferred characterisation of the early twenty-first century, since it draws attention to our inability to draw effective attention to anything.

Agency: for *beings* (q.v.); the capacity to take action towards a specific outcome, and thus to make judgments as to what actions and outcomes should be pursued. For things; the capacity to influence which actions or outcomes are pursued and thus affect the judgements of beings. See also *actor-network theory* (q.v.).

Agent-focused: any form of ethics in which the disposition and character of the person acting is the emphasized element, i.e. *virtue ethics* (q.v.). Compare *rule-focused* and *outcome-focused* (q.q.v.).

ANT: see *actor-network theory* (q.v.).

Being: an entity capable of imagining itself as existing within a world, and possessing a coherent narrative self. Almost all animals are 'beings' in this sense, and an argument can be made for plants too, but it is not clear whether *robots* (q.v.) could qualify.

Blind faith: the *debility* resulting from replacing *faith* with certainty, thus destroying *fidelity* (q.q.v.).

Bluntness: the *debility* (q.v.) associated with either a disregard for courtesy, or an obsessive truthfulness. Contrast *tact* (q.v.).

Chaos nova: a metaphor for our moral situation, drawing on Charles Taylor's idea of 'the nova effect', the near-infinite diversification of identities that resulted from the fracturing of *traditions* (q.v.), and Michael Moorcock's contrast between Law and Chaos.

Community: humans who are personally related in some way, such that they share a bond and knowledge of each other. This could be a geographic community, but there are also communities of practitioners in crafts, art, sport, research and so forth. See also *fidelity* (q.v.).

Consequentialism: a form of *outcome-focused* ethics (q.v.) that judges right and wrong solely by the *consequences* of acting. See also the *moral disaster of consequentialism* (q.v.).

Convivial: Ivan Illich's term for tools that foster individual competence and control (e.g. a hammer or bicycle). See also *conviviality* and *cyber-fidelity* (q.q.v.).

Conviviality: Ivan Illich's term for the quality of societies in which technology serves politically interrelated individuals. See also *convivial* (q.v.).

Cornerstone virtues: my term for Alasdair MacIntyre's trio of *virtues* that are central to maintaining any *practice* or *tradition*: *courage, justice,* and *honesty* (q.q.v.).

Courage: the *virtue* (q.v.) of taking action we feel ought to be taken but are afraid of pursuing. Compare *cyber-courage* and contrast *cyber-cowardice* (q.q.v).

Cruelty: the *debility* (q.v.) of acting towards other beings with the purposeful intent of hurting them. Compare *cyber-cruelty* (q.v.).

Cultural nomad: the condition of contemporary humans who are unbound by *tradition* (q.v.), and equate this with freedom. This book argues that this situation is not freedom but a kind of ephemeral prison.

Cyber-blunt: the quality of a robot that behaves inconsiderately in terms of what it displays or reveals, e.g. triggering gratuitous pop-ups. Contrast *cyber-tact* (q.v.).

Cyber-compulsion: the quality of a *robot* that grips the attention of its human, encouraging them to impulsively return their attention to it, also referred to as *cyber-itch* (q.q.v.). Contrast *cyber-restraint* (q.v.).

Cyber-courage: the quality of a *cyborg* such that it acts with *courage*, and of a *robot* such that it encourages this (q.q.v.). Contrast *cyber-cowardice* (q.v.).

Cyber-cowardice: the quality of a *cyborg* (q.v.) such that it acts as a bully or murderer, or otherwise hides behind technology to act with cowardice. Also, the quality of a *robot* (q.v.) such that it encourages this.

Cyber-cruelty: the quality of a *cyborg* such that it acts with *cruelty*, or of a *robot* (q.q.v.) that encourages this. Contrast *cyber-kindness* (q.v.).

Cyber-debilitating: a quality of a *robot* that encourages a moral *debility* (q.q.v.) in a human.

Cyber-deceitful: the quality of a *cyborg* that intentionally misrepresents something to others, i.e. that engages in *false witness* (q.q.v.). Also, a hypothetical defect of a *robot* (q.v.) that intentionally misrepresents something to its human.

Cyber-dependence: the quality of a *cyberg*, or a *robot* produced by a cyberg, that means its human is bound to the cyberg rather than any *community* (q.q.v.). Contrast *cyber-fidelity* (q.v.).

Cyber-disdain: the quality of a *cyborg* (q.v.) that ignores the individual needs of others. Also, the quality of a *robot* (q.v.) that either encourages this, or acts without the consent of its human. Compare *disdain*, contrast *cyber-respect*, and note the overlap with *cyber-indignance* (q.q.v.).

Cyber-domination: the quality of a *robot* (q.v.) that encourages a human to persist in a task that the robot determines e.g. slot machines tend to be cyber-dominant over humans. Compare *cyber-submission* and contrast *cyber-tenacity* (q.q.v.).

Cyber-fidelity: the quality of a *cyborg* that aids its commitment to *practices* and their *communities* (q.q.v). Also, the quality of a *robot* that encourages this without engendering any additional dependence upon itself; another name for *convivial* (q.q.v.). Compare *fidelity* and contrast *cyber-dependence* (q.q.v.).

Cyberfetish: the exaltation of technology, and in its more extreme manifestations, a longing to physically merge with technology.

Cyber-gullible: the quality of a *cyborg* such that it tends to propagate what has been claimed by others without confirming that the account entails *reliable witness* (q.q.v.). Also, the quality of a *robot* that encourages this. Compare *gullible* and contrast *cyber-honest* (q.q.v.).

Cyber-honest: the quality of a *cyborg* such that anything it repeats entails *reliable witness* (q.q.v.). Also, the hypothetical quality of a *robot* that encourages this.

Cyber-indignance: the quality of a *cyborg* such that it pursues reprehensible vigilante actions (e.g. death threats), or elicits *cyber-disdain* in the form of tirades of disgust that the cyborg justifies through appeal to their own *ideals of justice* (q.q.v.). Also, the quality of a *robot* (q.v.) that encourages this. Compare *indignance* and contrast *cyber-just* (q.q.v.).

Cyber-itch: a synonym for *cyber-compulsion* (q.v.).

Cyber-just: the quality of a *cyborg* that acts upon its *ideals of justice* without *cyber-indignance* (q.q.v.). Also, the quality of a *robot* that (perhaps only hypothetically) encourages this, or that upholds justice in relation to its human (for example, through adequate password protection). Contrast *cyber-nihil-*

ism and *cyber-indignance* (q.q.v.).

Cyber-kindness: the quality of a *cyborg* (q.v.) that acts compassionately towards others. Also, the quality of a *robot* that either encourages this or protects its human from unfortunate events (e.g. the desktop recycling bin protects against accidental deletion). Compare *kindness* and contrast *cyber-cruelty* (q.q.v.).

Cyber-nihilism: the quality of a *robot* (q.v.) that causes it to act towards its human with complete disregard for any moral considerations, e.g. a computer virus. Compare *nihilism* (q.v.).

Cyber-respect: the quality of a *cyborg* (q.v.) such that it takes into account the individual needs of others. Also, the quality of a *robot* (q.v.) that either encourages this, or allows its human to consent to what it is doing. Compare *respect* and contrast *cyber-disdain* (q.q.v.).

Cyber-restraint: the quality of a *cyborg* (q.v.) such that it is careful about acting upon compulsive impulse, especially with respect to engagement with technologically-mediated activities. Also, the rare or non-existent quality of a *robot* (q.v.) which does not encourage its human to act compulsively towards it. Compare *restraint* and contrast *cyber-compulsion* or *cyber-itch* (q.q.v.).

Cyber-submission: what a human does when they yield to a robot's *cyber-domination* (q.v.). This is a rare case where the prefix 'cyber-' is being used to describe a human *debility* (q.v.), the point being that in such instances it is a quality of the *robot* that creates the relevant circumstances.

Cyber-tact: the quality of a *cyborg* (q.v.) that takes into account the emotional impact of action or speech upon others. Also, the (hypothetical) quality of a *robot* (q.v.) that encourages this, or (more commonly) that acts considerately towards their humans in terms of the triggering of information. Contrast *cyber-blunt* (q.v.).

Cyber-tenacity: the quality of a *cyborg* (q.v.) to persist in a task that it chooses for itself. Also, the quality of a *robot* (q.v.) that encourages this. Contrast *cyber-domination* and *cyber-submission* (q.q.v.).

Cybervirtue: the desirable qualities of a *cyborg*, both in terms of the robot's relationship with its human, referred to as *programmed cybervirtue*, or the human-robot cyborg's relationship with other humans or cyborgs, termed *social cybervirtue* (q.q.v.). See also *personal cybervirtue* (q.v.).

Cybervirtuous: possessing *cybervirtue* (q.v.).

Cyberg: the cybernetic networks that connect beings and things into vast and complex webs of connectivity, beyond our capacity to mentally envisage. This term can be applied to very different kinds of networks, including technologies, nations, social networks, and even money. The term combines '*cyborg*' (q.v.) and 'iceberg', making reference to the idea that you can only see 10% of an iceberg from the surface of the sea. See also *shallow-sighted* (q.v.).

Cyborg: any combination of beings and things that acts with a greater range of possibilities than either can achieve alone, typically in this book a human-robot pairing.

Debility: a moral failure of habit, what was classically termed a vice. Since this latter term has come to be associated with various specific illegal activities such as drugs and prostitution, this book uses debility or *defect* (q.v.) in place of vice.

Deceitfulness: the *debility* (q.v.) of intentionally engaging in or propagating *false witness* (q.q.v.) i.e. of intentionally misrepresenting what one has witnessed or understood. Contrast *honesty* (q.v.).

Deep-sighted: the opposite of *shallow-sighted* (q.v.), implying a capacity to see into the vastly complex cybernetic networks we are enmeshed within. See also *cyberg* (q.v.).

Defect: a moral failure caused by the absence of any sensitivity to a particular ethical concern. Contrast *debility* (q.v.).

Deontology. see *duty ethics* (q.v.).

Digital public space: any computer-mediated service where people present themselves publically, including all social networks (Facebook, Twitter, Pinterest etc.), news or video sharing sites (e.g. YouTube, Dailymotion etc.) that accept comments, shopping websites where reviews can be posted, and so forth.

Digital robot: a *robot* (q.v.) operating on binary instructions, usually with silicon chips e.g. a laptop, a PC, a smartphone. In this book, the 'digital' will often be omitted, since most robots today are of this kind.

Disdain: the *debility* of acting towards other humans with an absence of *respect* (q.q.v.), usually constrained to the context of people the human in question finds morally disgusting.

Dissensus: Jacques Rancière's concept that politics requires the recognition of disagreement, or else it cannot be a space for discussing how to live together but only an empty power struggle to enforce a pre-conceived consensus.

Duty ethics: a form of *rule-focused* ethics (q.v.) that judges the permissibility of actions in terms of duties to act out or refrain from acting, also known as 'deontology'. Compare *virtue ethics* and *consequentialism* (q.q.v.).

Fact: an assertion that can be made reliably (and that can be verified), which emerges from the refinement of a kind of *knowledge* (q.v.).

Faith: a disposition towards uncertainty whereby trust is maintained in the absence of unequivocal grounds to do so. See also *fidelity*, which is the *virtue* of having faith and avoiding *blind faith* (q.q.v.).

False witness: presenting a claim that does not entail the reliability of authentic knowledge. Contrast *reliable witness* (q.v.).

Fidelity: the *virtue* (q.v.) of loyalty to a person, institution, practice, or ideal. See also *faith* (q.v.).

Free-to-play: a business model for videogames that offers the software for free, but asks users to pay *micro-transactions* (q.v.) for certain abilities or actions.

Gigacyberg: a *cyberg* (q.v.) with at least a billion entities enmeshed within it (using the short scale, or a thousand million on the traditional long scale). Compare *kilocyberg* and *megacyberg* (q.q.v.).

Gullible: the *debility* (q.v.) of a human who does not confirm whether what they are repeating was presented reliably to them, especially as a result of accepting any claim that happens to align with their values. See also *false witness* and *reliable witness* (q.q.v.). Compare *cyber-gullible* (q.v.).

Habit: whatever beings undertake repeatedly, such that it becomes easier to do so again and thus a skill develops wherever there is the possibility of expertise. In this book, *virtue* (q.v.) is defined as a moral habit.

Honesty: the *virtue* of being a *reliable witness* (q.q.v.), both for what has been personally witnessed, and for what is repeated in respect to others. Compare *cyber-honest* and contrast *deceitfulness* and *gullible* (q.q.v.).

Ideals of justice: the conceptual basis of anyone's concept of justice in terms of imagined 'oughts' e.g. equality, fairness, restitution.

Indignance: the *debility* resulting from *blind faith* in specific *ideals of justice*, resulting in *disdain* or *cruelty* (q.q.v.) towards others who may or not share these ideals. Contrast *just* (q.v.).

Infidelity: betrayal of one's former loyalty to a person, institution, practice, or ideal. Contrast *fidelity* (q.v.).

Internet troll: see *troll* (q.v.).

Just: the *virtue* of upholding *ideals of justice* (q.q.v.) as guides to a particular human's behaviour. Compare *cyber-just* and contrast *nihilism* or *indignance* (q.q.v).

Justice: see *just* for the virtue and *ideals of justice* (q.q.v.) for the concept that this depends upon.

Kilocyberg: a *cyberg* (q.v.) with at least a thousand entities enmeshed within it. Compare *megacyberg* and *gigacyberg* (q.q.v.).

Kindness: the *virtue* (q.v.) of providing support for others, through forgiveness, generosity, helpfulness, peace-making etc. Compare *cyber-kindness* and contrast *cyber-cruelty* (q.q.v.).

Knowledge: any *practice* that can be performed with a degree of reliability and that allows for the assertion of *facts* (q.q.v.) as a side effect of its execution.

Machine-mind: a term from the Taoist sage Chuang Tzu that implies a change of mindset when we start using machinery to work for us. See also *machine worries* and *standing reserve* (q.q.v.).

Machine worries: the Taoist sage Chaung Tzu's term, which highlights the problems of participating with devices. A machine may make a specific task easier to execute, but then the problems of the machine (maintenance, repair, increased pace of work etc.) can eclipse our own engagement with the underlying experience.

Megacyberg: a *cyberg* (q.v.) with at least a million entities enmeshed within it. Compare *kilocyberg* and *gigacyberg* (q.q.v.).

Metaphysics: that which cannot be tested or proven, i.e. claims concerning reality that exceed experience or direct evidence. See also *mythos* (q.v.).

Micro-transaction: an online payment for a small amount of money, typically an amount payable in coins if this were a cash payment.

Moral disaster: see *moral disaster of individualism* and *moral dis-*

aster of consequentialism (q.q.v.).

Moral disaster of consequentialism: the corruption of *outcome-focused ethics* such that morality is reduced to mere mathematical calculations, particularly in the contexts of corporate financial decision making and justifications in terms of the purported *utility* (q.q.v.) of new technology.

Moral disaster of individualism: the elevation of selfishness to a moral principle under the guise of 'freedom' (e.g. the suspicious association of capitalist markets with personal liberty), or the application of a paternalistic enforcement of 'morality' that denies freedoms of various kinds while claiming to be defending the freedom of others (e.g. all forms of political correctness).

Moral horror: cognitive dissonance in the context of ethical judgements, i.e. a psychological inability to assess a topic once we are disgusted by it.

Moral representation: shared reflection on our ethical values and judgements (e.g. Catholic confession, debate in a jury room, or friends discussing a dilemma in the pub).

Mutual respect: the agreement between individuals to respect one another's individuality arising from our shared rationality, expressed in Kant's philosophy as a facet of the fundamental principle of morality.

Mythos: a collection of imaginative patterns that underlie a particular perspective on existence.

Nihilism: the *debility* (q.v.) resulting from a self-defeating faith that there is nothing worth having faith in. Clearly, if this were true it would not be possible to uphold nihilism without being caught in a contradiction. Compare *cyber-nihilism* and contrast *just* (q.q.v.).

Nova: see *chaos nova* (q.v.).

Outcome-focused: any form of ethics in which the consequences of actions are used to judge their moral worth e.g. *consequentialism* (q.v.). Compare *agent-focused* and *rule-focused* (q.q.v.).

Personal cybervirtue: another name for the virtue of the human part of a cyborg in so much as it is exercised within the framework of specific cybernetic networks.

Practice: an activity that becomes more reliable through its exercise, and that is shared by some *community* (q.v.). All skills and competences can be understood as practices, even moral competences such as *virtues* (q.v.).

Programmed cybervirtue: the qualities of a *robot* in dealing with its human (when they form a *cyborg* together) that resemble traditional *virtue* (q.q.v.). This is also called the internal sense of cybervirtue, because it is internal to the human-robot pairing of the relevant cyborg.

Public karma system: a designed system for tracking behaviour, such that positive (or negative) behaviour accumulates as a score.

Radical monopoly: Ivan Illich's term for a situation whereby one kind of industrial product exercises exclusive control of the satisfaction of some need e.g. cars possess a radical monopoly on transportation, since almost all nations develop road infrastructures in preference to more egalitarian alternatives such as bicycles.

Reliable witness: Speaking on behalf of someone else without distorting what they would say, or being part of a chain of speakers passing on claims reliably. In Isabelle Stengers' sense of this term, researchers with viable experimental methods turn inanimate objects into reliable witnesses through application of the *knowledge* entailed in their research *practices* (q.q.v.).

Respect: the *virtue* (q.v.) of treating others as individual beings with their own plans, needs, and values. Compare *cyber-respect* and contrast *cyber-disdain* (q.q.v.). See also *mutual respect* (q.v.).

Restraint: the *virtue* (q.v.) of heeding good reasons to refrain from acting, rather than giving into a desire to do otherwise. Compare *cyber-restraint* and contrast *cyber-itch* (q.q.v.).

Robot: any device capable of independent functioning, such as a steam engine, a jukebox, or a smartphone, the last of which is also an example of a *digital robot* (q.v.). The term 'robot' in this book typically refers to a digital robot, and the 'digital' is thus frequently omitted.

Rule-focused: any form of ethic in which the emphasized element concerns rules (or rights) to be complied with e.g. *duty ethics*. (q.v.). Compare *agent-focused* and *outcome-focused* (q.q.v.).

Semi-presence: the state of being focused upon a digital robot (q.v.) in a situation when attention also or primarily needs to be in the world around the human, e.g. texting while driving.

Shaduf: an irrigation device, known since at least ancient Egypt, consisting of a pole mounted upon a fulcrum that is used to lift water from a well in a bucket through the use of a counterweight.

Shallow-sighted: the problem that our cybernetic networks or *cybergs* (q.v.) are vast and complex, and we only tend to notice the 'surface' (the 'tip of the cyberg') i.e. the technology as it presents itself to us. We see cars and drivers, but do not think about the network required to make that technology viable.

Social cybervirtue: the qualities of a *cyborg* in dealing with other cyborgs (or humans) that resemble traditional *virtue* (q.q.v.). This is also called the external sense of cybervirtue, because it is external to the human-robot pairing of the relevant cyborg.

Smartphone: a compulsively designed *digital robot* (q.v.) that presents itself as merely a telephone.

Smartphone zombie: a *cyborg* who has surrendered to the compulsive qualities of *smartphones* (q.q.v.).

Standing reserve: Heidegger's term for how the natural world is perceived once it is understood as resources, and not as a living environment. Compare *machine-mind* (q.v.).

Stultification: Jacques Rancière's term for any form of education where the learner is forced to understand a topic (or learn a skill) in a particular way, rather than being encouraged to develop their own competence through any viable method.

Tact: a *virtue* (q.v.) of attentiveness to the emotional impact of speech and behaviour. Compare *cyber-tact* and contrast *bluntness* and *tactlessness* (q.q.v).

Tactlessness: the *defect* corresponding to absence of *tact* (q.q.v.), and therefore a lack of awareness of the emotional impact of speech and behaviour.

Tenacity: the *virtue* (q.v.) of diligently pursuing what has been willed, as opposed to submitting to moment-to-moment impulses.

Thing: any and all entities that lack the qualities defining *beings* (q.v.).

Tradition: any human activity with a specific focus, set of methods and its own values can be considered a tradition. E.g. cartography, chess, chemistry, Christianity, cooperage, crochet. This term is broadly equivalent to Isabelle Stengers' use of the term *practice* (q.v.).

Troll: a *cyborg* that acts with both cruelty and cowardice to bully other cyborgs (q.v.). It is argued in this book that the qualities of *robots* in terms of *cyber-cruelty* and *cyber-cowardice* (q.q.v.) effectively encourage trolls to act in this way.

Unmarriage: stable, committed, romantic relationships that have not entailed a marriage ceremony or equivalent act of public promising.

Utility: the capacity to bring about desired outcomes, and hence a highly desirable quality in all new technology. In this book, utility is viewed as an aspect of the *moral disaster of consequentialism* (q.v.).

Virtue: the positive, desirable, or meritorious *habits* (q.v.) of beings such as humans.

Virtue ethics: a form of *agent-focused* ethics in which what is good is judged in terms of the qualities of agents i.e. virtues (q.q.v.). Compare *duty ethics* and *consequentialism* (q.q.v.).

Virtuous: possessing *virtue* (q.v.).

Well sweep: see *shaduf* (q.v.).

Will: the capacity to act decisively towards goals or desires.

AUTHOR NOTES

Why this Book Has No Citations

While I hope academics will enjoy this book, I have not written it primarily for scholars. With that in mind, I decided to omit citations from the main text entirely and try something different. Have no fear, all the references are dutifully catalogued at the end of the text, but to link up my sources to these I have chosen to use this 'Author Notes' appendix as a guide. I have provided the names of the texts and their year of publication the first time they are referenced in these notes, after which I just refer to the name of the text. This not only leaves the individual chapters clean of clutter and thus more readable, it means I can say more about the relationship of my work to its inspirations for those who care about such things. If the citation and referencing systems were developed by universities to help scholars be more reliable witnesses, I hope this method makes me a more thorough witness in respect of my own work, and the dependencies and debts I owe to others who went before me.

Why Some People Are Addressed by Their First Names

It is now traditional in journal papers and the like to treat other academics as mere coded resources by reducing their first name to an impersonal initial. I dislike this. I prefer to remember that my work has been aided by specific humans with names and lives. I detest the attitude that crept in during the twentieth century whereby scientific writing (and the bad habits there have now spread into the humanities, where they are utterly out of place) must pretend to be a cold and distant voice of truth. Nothing could distort academic work more than to elide its human – all too human – foundations. In this book, I have gone a step further: when I happen to know the cyborg I am talking about, I have referred to them by their first name. This is not only more polite, it acknowledges my personal relationship with them to the reader. This strikes me as a far more honest approach than the make-believe game whereby acting as if academics were mere objects allows us to pretend to be objective.

Chapter I
Living with Machines

The idea of a robot as a machine with autonomous function originates in my own *Chaos Ethics* (2014), Chapter 1, section 'Cyberfetish', while Ivan Illich's concepts of *conviviality* or *convivial tools* can be found in his 1973 book *Tools for Conviviality*. Donna Haraway's remarkable polemic 'The Cyborg Manifesto' was republished as part of a collection in 1991, although I'll wager if you enter her name and that title into a search engine it will deliver you unto the relevant prose. It is unfortunate, in some respects, that this is the essay that made her name, since it has somewhat obscured her other work. I shall attempt to address this deficit of attention later in this book.

What is Cybervirtue?

The moral implications of tools and objects is a contemporary topic with a wealth of literature accreting around it, but great places to start are the essays I have referenced below by Bruno Latour (2002), Peter-Paul Verbeek (2006), or Isabelle Stengers (2012). Discussion of these papers, and upon the topic of the moral implications of tools in general, is also a major aspect of my own *Chaos Ethics*.

Graham Harman's views in this regard can be found in his doctoral thesis on Heidegger's concepts of readiness-to-hand and presence-at-hand, *Tool-Being* (1999), later a book in its own right, but to get rapidly to the ethical implications of this I recommend Lucas Introna's 'Ethics and the speaking of things' (2009), which makes the key point that our ignoring of the importance of things was allowing us to act in quite atrocious ways that now need reconsidering. As for Martin Heidegger himself, see the notes for the next chapter.

For a primer on virtue ethics, its history, practice, and difference from other forms of ethical thought, there is no-one better to turn to than Alasdair MacIntyre. *After Virtue: A Study in Moral Theory* (1984) is the essential starting place and turned out to be a huge influence upon me, although I did not realise it at the time. If you've already read this, *Three Rival Versions of Moral Enquiry* (1990) is a fascinating exposition of MacIntyre's account of virtue ethics and the flaws in other approaches to morality, which substantially informs and supports my argumentation within this book.

Regarding the effects of writing technology upon the Athenians, Stefano Gualeni discusses this in Chapter 6 of his *Virtual Worlds as Philosophical Tools* (2015). His discussion intends to defend our use of computers, while still acknowledging the trade-offs involved in accepting their use, much as Socrates concedes to writing in Plato's *Phaedrus* dialogue. Stefano's book borders on being an apologetics for technology, but shares with this book the view that it is important to recognise the mutual influence humans and computers may have on one another.

Smartphone Zombies

The AFP article (2014) referred to appears to be the locus of dissemination for the term 'smartphone zombie', since it was covered in a huge number of news outlets at the time. I have found a few earlier uses, however, e.g. Nicole Saidi (2012) used the phrase in a joking response to an article by comedian Dean Obeidallah (2012) where he reported his own difficulty in going a day without his cell phone. The discussion of the 'head-down tribe' comes from an article by Mark Sharp (2015), raising very similar concerns (and reporting remarkably similar incidents) to the earlier AFP piece.

For the argument that this is the Age of Distraction, see my short-form philosophy book *Wikipedia Knows Nothing* (2016), and for statistics on 'distracted driving' see the US Department of Transportation website (2016) and the CDC's website (2016). I got the term 'telephone obedience' from Babette Babich, who discusses it in her lectures on 'virtual friends'. For discussion of our relationship with telephones, see Grant Noble (1987) and Ann Moyal (1989), two distinguished Australian researchers who contributed to communication studies at a time when many had not even considered it a viable field of enquiry.

The idea that European language philosophy (as opposed to, say, Chinese, Indian, or Japanese philosophy) is inescapably conditioned by the Greeks is developed in careful detail by Gilles Deleuze and Félix Guattari in *What is Philosophy?* (1991). A more concise summary comes to us from Alfred North Whitehead's (1929) remark that the European philosophical tradition is just a series of footnotes to Plato.

Chapter II
Machine Worries
I am indebted to both Ed Key, co-creator of the astonishing artgame *Proteus* (2012), and Phyllis Mazzocchi, for introducing

me to the philosophy of Chuang Tzu and his 'free and blithe-some wanderings'. The story recounted at the start in my own phrasing is from section 12 of the *Chuang Tzu*, and draws against the Burton Watson translation (1968). This story also appears in a paper by George Teschner and Alessandro Tomasi (2009) to illustrate the relationship between Heidegger's philosophy and Taoist thought. This connection is explored in great detail by Tom Delaune in 'The Tao of Heidegger' (2015). I'm indebted to both sources for my discussion here, although Delaune's account is the place to go if the interest is in Heidegger's connection to Taoism.

Heidegger's 'The Question Concerning Technology' (1954) is foundational for this section, and has an excellent translation by William Lovitt (1977). Alas, it is far from an easy read, and certainly not recommended for anyone who shies away from Continental philosophy, which requires a certain commitment to engage with fully. However, a great summary of Heidegger's thoughts on this topic is Mark Blitz's 'Understanding Heidegger on Technology' (2014), which cuts through Heidegger's challenging terminology and makes clear the essential points of his thought. For the destruction of rainforests in order to grow commodity crops (primarily palm oil), see the report by environmental group Mighty (2016), or just type 'palm oil' and 'rainforest' into a search engine.

My preferred translation of the *Tao Te Ching* is by Arthur Waley (1954), and the discussion of the 'Three Treasures' can be found in Chapter 67. Yanxia Zhao has written an illuminating piece 'The Spirit of Charity and Compassion in Daoist Religion' (2015) that helpfully contextualises the relationship between the Three Treasures, and although its focus is Confucian teachings (which are sometimes viewed as rivals to Taoism, despite their practical coexistence in lived Chinese culture), James T. Bretzke's essay 'The Tao of Confucian Virtue Ethics' (1995) is a great starting place for anyone interested in placing Chinese virtue traditions into dialogue with their Western analogues.

Regarding the games mentioned in this section, my work frequently draws reference to the pivotal tabletop role-playing game *Dungeons & Dragons* by Gary Gygax and Dave Arneson (1974), and a detailed discussion of its history and influence appears in my *Imaginary Games* (2011). *Minecraft* (2009) was begun by Marcus 'Notch' Persson and later continued by Jens Bergensten, and eventually by a larger team. Its colossal success appears to have become a burden for Notch, who seems relieved to have sold his company, Mojang, to Microsoft for the absurd sum of $2.5 billion. Here is yet another dimension of 'machine worries'.

Respectful Robots

What I call 'mutual respect' in *Chaos Ethics* is Kant's second formulation of the categorical imperative, which he discusses as part of his *Groundwork for the Metaphysics of Morals* (1785). This is usually termed the Formula of Humanity as End in Itself, making the point that we should not simply use other humans as means, but always as ends in their own right. Relatedly, Heidegger's 'The Question Concerning Technology' warns about the risk of treating humans as mere resources as a consequence of our attitude to technology as mere utility.

Carol Cadwalladr's piece for *The Observer*, 'Google, democracy and the truth about internet search' (2016), exposes a significant problem with internet search suggestions: it is possible to lead people to answers that are established by aggregation of links, and therefore topics can be dominated by anyone who sets out to abuse the search algorithms in this way. Her examples run from typing 'are Jews' and being offered 'are Jews evil?' as an option, which leads to various right-wing sites that make this disturbing claim. She provides various other examples such as 'are Muslims bad?' and 'was Hitler bad?' that run along similar lines.

The Unkindness of Strangers

The concept of moral horror that is introduced here is defined and explained within Chapter 5 of *Chaos Ethics*, and is in effect merely Leon Festinger's cognitive dissonance (1957) applied in the specific context of morality. I prefer the term 'moral horror' as I find it alludes to the phenomena in question more elegantly than the subtle distancing of the term 'cognitive dissonance'. Here as elsewhere in psychology, extravagant terms seem to lend objective credence – yet pragmatically, the terminology isn't what makes Festinger's work so compelling, but rather the impeccable research behind it. I think it worth cutting the number of syllables in half to get this idea across more easily.

Charles Taylor's term 'the Nova effect' appears in his mammoth work *A Secular Age* (2007), and my discussion of this can be found in *Imaginary Games*. For *The Virtuous Cyborg*, I talk about 'the chaos nova', combining Taylor's concept with Michael Moorcock's metaphysical contrast between Law and Chaos. These were developed in his existentialist novels, which include the multiple fantasy series that are collectively known as the Eternal Champion sagas. This is also the origin of the name *Chaos Ethics*, as that book makes extremely clear (see especially Chapter 3, section 'Moorcock's Mythology').

I provide arguments against the indiscriminate use of masks in *Wikipedia Knows Nothing*, although my position in that particular book was primarily looking at the abuse of power facilitated by anonymity. I still allowed the possibility of there being legitimate reasons for someone to want anonymity, and merely disputed those that were advanced in the context of both Wikipedia and double blind peer review. In the next chapter of this book, the idea of 'anonymity' itself is more closely dissected.

Chapter III
Lessons from the MUD

Brian Green's (2017) discussions of anonymity and privacy provide an excellent overview of the issues, as well as making clear what is at stake in enforcing public identities in terms of reducing privacy. Brian agrees that scale is the most significant factor distinguishing between the MUDs (which mostly worked well as communities) and contemporary digital public spaces (which are significant sites of abuse at the moment). He does point out, however, that the MUD communities were mostly comprised of nerdy university students, which helped reduce the culture clash problems highlighted later in this chapter.

However, Brian disagrees on my emphasis on *alone* and *unknown* anonymity. He contends abuse is primarily a socially-motivated problem, with the focus on the mob as the initiating force. While mob abuse is certainly something that happens, and cyborgs frequently appear emboldened in writing abusive comments when others have already done so, I remain convinced that a significant number of problematic cyborgs act alone, and that the conditions of effective unknowabilty make these situations worse in the open internet. In this regard, I would point to street harassment (Kearl, 2014) where women report 70% of incidents entail a lone male harasser, and to a Pew report (Duggan, 2014) that suggests two thirds of people did not know the identity of their online abusers, primarily because they were complete strangers. I suspect if and when further research takes place that bears on this issue it will reveal that both kinds of abuse coexist, and that the situation cannot easily be boiled down to a single problem.

Richard Bartle, who along with Roy Trubshaw created the world's first multi-user dungeon, MUD1 (1978), mentioned to me in connection with the original draft of this piece that he had long since concluded that smaller communities were the best option, all things considered, for MMO games. In the context of the size of 'shards' (community segments of a massively multiplayer game), he argues in *MMOs from the Outside In* (2015) that there is a difficult to determine balance point between a large enough community to make the game an attractive proposition for players, and a small enough community to avoid the hassles that come with scale. This very much supports the arguments I make here, although he shrugged his virtual shoulders as to how far the methods of the MMO could be extended into social media.

Sherry Turkle's ground-breaking research on the social effects of computer-mediated communication can be found in her book *Alone Together* (2011). Alas, Turkle's work has not had the impact it deserves, except perhaps to extend the ongoing divide between so-called 'Millennials', who have grown up with digital public spaces and thus find their situation perfectly normal, and those of us who have lived through the transition and are somewhat concerned about what has occurred. Turkle's work is grounded on thorough-going empirical studies: to dismiss it outright is merely an act of denial.

Finally, the concept of a player practice that I allude to here, and the lineages of play that connect games historically through the conservation of player practices, is outlined in a number of places in my academic papers including 'No-one Plays Alone' (2016c) and 'Game Design Lineages: *Minecraft*'s Inventory', which I wrote with my good and excellent academic friend José Zagal (2017).

Should Your Laptop Say Please?

Brian's friend Randy Farmer, along with Bryce Glass, have written an excellent how-to guide for constructing web reputation systems, including public karma systems, logically entitled *Building Web Reputation Systems* (2010). Frankly, if you stick 'Randy Farmer' and 'Public Karma' into a search engine, you have an excellent chance of hitting some of the wealth of material he has provided on this topic, although if you actually intend to explore this kind of software robot you ought to consider going straight for the book as right now there's nothing to beat it.

Tenacity and the Domination of Things

Bruno Latour's reflections on the role of objects in agency can be found in a great many places, although the standard reference for what is called actor-network theory (ANT) is perhaps *Reassembling the Social* (2005). The example of the cigarette and its smoker is discussed in *Politics of Nature* (1999), a text that I find receives less attention than others in Latour's 'canon', but which has been extremely influential upon my own work, including this book. I would probably even recommend this over some of the more obvious suggestions as an intriguing place to begin an encounter with Latour's work.

I have a sustained discussion of the Enlightenment concept of 'will' in my discussion of Kant's moral thought in *Chaos Ethics*, Chapter 7: Rights and Wrongs. In this, as in all discussion of Kant, I am indebted to Christine Korsgaard (e.g.

1997) and especially to Allen Wood (e.g. 1999, 2008), whose wonderful translations and clarifications of Kant's work drew me in to a love of Kant that has never left me. I dispute anyone's suggestion that Kant's ethics are no longer relevant to contemporary situations: anyone who thinks this way has not adequately understood Kant's work, and should make a beeline to Allen Wood's work for clarification and elucidation. In particular, I do not see how anyone can be a defender of human rights and not think Kant's moral philosophy supremely relevant, especially today when few nations are standing by their promises in this regard.

The concept of 'schedules of reinforcement' dates back to experiments by the Behaviourists Charles Ferster and B.F. Skinner (1957). Although Behaviourism now seems a somewhat fanciful philosophy of behaviour, the concept of schedules of reinforcement remains extremely pertinent – and indeed, is taught in some places as a means of understanding game design. I myself caught a talk of this kind the first time I was on the faculty of the Game Developer's Conference. I guess it's not really a surprise: even in the earliest days of the 8-bit videogames, calling a game 'addictive' was considered a positive ascription.

As mentioned in the main text, Jacques Rancière's discussion of 'stultification' can be found in *The Ignorant Schoolmaster* (1987). In essence, when someone forces you to learn a skill or understand a subject *in the same way they do*, you are suffering from stultification. The point is that authentic learning is to acquire the capability, and nothing about this requires that you learn it or understand it *the same way someone else does*. I was immediately struck by the way that gamification (the process of putting game-like structures into work environments) was effectively stultification, and indeed that systems such as achievements in games *were also* stultification – that we were suffering from the absurd situation of the gamification-of-games. I presented this idea at the *Work and Play* conference in Salford (2016b), and will be writing the paper about this when this book's manuscript is completed, although both Sebastian Detarding and José Zagal inform me others have already written papers with somewhat similar perspectives within game studies.

Raph Koster's conception of fun as learning appears in *A Theory of Fun for Game Design* (2005). Although I find that Raph's concept of 'fun' has been truncated and massaged rather excessively to support his otherwise implausible suggestion that 'fun is learning', he is nonetheless extremely insightful regarding the importance of learning to the play of games. As for Jane McGonigal, her book *Reality is Broken* (2011) offers an extremely positive stance on the benefits of videogames, and the possibilities posed by bringing these advantages into everyday life. As is probably evident from the discussions in this section of the book, I am far more critical about this topic. Nonetheless, I still concur with her assessment that there are opportunities here that other kinds of technology have not afforded.

Chapter IV
Tip of the Cyberg

As mentioned in the notes for the previous chapter, a good introduction to actor-network theory (ANT) is Latour's *Reassembling the Social* (2005). The definition of ANT that is most commonly cited is by John Law (2009), and I have used this here in outlining the core concept behind this sociological method. I am less interested in ANT as a form of sociology than I am the philosophical implications set in motion by this way of thinking. ANT is part of a recent movement in philosophy that in *Chaos Ethics* is termed 'secular animism'. It is not a coincidence that I have drawn against Taoism in this book, since this Eastern philosophical tradition also entails a form of animism.

An extended discussion of the way we fantasise about technology can also be found in *Chaos Ethics*, particularly in the section 'Cyberfetish', in Chapter 1, and the role of science fiction as a contemporary mythos is explored in *The Mythology of Evolution* (2012), Chapter 5, section 'Orthodox Science Fiction'. In both cases, my work has built upon that of Mary Midgley, particularly *Evolution as a Religion* (1985) and *Science as Salvation* (1992). I am also indebted to Mary for her correspondence, which has been both supportive and challenging of my ideas. She is surely Britain's greatest living philosopher, and even at 97 years of age she remains a force of nature, and a constant inspiration to me in attempting to write philosophy in an accessible style.

Arthur C. Clarke's 'Third Law' appears in his essay 'Hazards of Prophecy: The Failure of Imagination' (1962). I have frequent cause to wonder what Clarke, who is perhaps the only futurist to have achieved any credibility (having predicted – and thus invented – the geostationary satellite in 1945), would have made of our contemporary situation.

Bruno Latour's adage that Boeing 747s don't fly, it is the airlines that fly, first made in 'On Technical Mediation' (1994), succinctly makes the general point that frames this discussion of cybergs. As noted above, this entire chapter depends upon Latour's thoughts on actor-network theory, and I must apologise to Michel Callon for not having read him yet, given his role in establishing this field.

I also have to acknowledge Graham Harman, Levi

Bryant, Timothy Morton, and Ian Bogost, whose work in object-oriented ontology (OOO) pings off, with, and against Latour into interesting spaces, and whose blogs I nibble at from time to time. Alas, I have not yet managed to read an entire book by any of them on this particular subject (sorry folks!) but I can attest to a wealth of interesting thought going on under the somewhat unwieldy banner of OOO. After ANT, OOO is probably the other key movement within secular animism.

I suspect part of my problem in terms of not engaging directly with OOO is that Ian is the only game designer-philosopher whose public profile outstrips mine, and I feel a certain pressure to keep at least some conceptual space between us, even if the *zeitgeist* has us swimming in similar pools from time to time. Besides, like Terence Blake, I am drawn to arguing *against* the tenets of the approach, although unlike Terence I haven't yet read enough of their work to give them a good fight.

Scaling Our Cybernetic Networks

In this section, all of the numbers and estimates were put together on the basis of a variety of ad hoc sources located using search engines. I have not referenced any of these sources: there seems little point. Even by the time this book makes it into print, all the numbers will have changed. The point is not the actual numbers, after all, but a sense of the scale of these networks. In this regard, I could see little point in treating what I have put here as 'research', in need of accurate references and data, preferring instead to see it as an informal discussion that helps clarify the implications of the cyberg concept introduced at the start of this chapter. Grumbling academics with impeachable credentials who feel I am cheating in this regard are entitled to denounce my lazy scholarship, if they wish.

Beyond Futile Outrage

The discussion here is pursued in far greater depth in *Chaos Ethics*. In brief, I identify in that book three different styles of ethical thought: the focus on actions in deontology (duty ethics, or rule-focused ethics), the focus on outcomes in Consequentialism (outcome-focused ethics), and the focus on the qualities of agents in virtue ethics (agent-focused ethics). I further argue that these are the only three possible perspectives on morality, because of the grammar of language, and that all three are valuable and important. Among the many discussions in that particular book is a detailed investigation of 'Who Killed Morality?' (Chapter 2) that informs what I'm presenting here.

Jonathan Haidt, whose work is brilliantly outside of the crippling liberal-conservative divide yet maddeningly narrow-minded at the same time, originally made his social intuitionalist claims in 'The Emotional Dog and its Rational Tail' (2001). J.W. Gray's review of this (2011) gives excellent pushback, and I engage with Haidt – sometimes in support, oftentimes on the offensive – throughout *Chaos Ethics*. The only time I've ever been more frustrated with an academic was Richard Dawkins, but in both cases (Haidt and Dawkins) having someone strident to argue against has been a tremendous asset to me. (My view of Dawkins is fully encapsulated within *The Mythology of Evolution*; when he stays on topic he is very good at explaining complex evolutionary topics, though.)

Alasdair MacIntyre's extensive and exemplary work on virtue ethics is discussed in the Author Notes for Chapter 1, as is Kant's work. MacIntyre's *After Virtue* has perhaps the best critique of the failures of 'rights talk' that can be found, although I have some critique of his views within *Chaos Ethics*. John Stewart Mill's key text is *On Liberty* (1859), and my discussion therein is – unsurprisingly – in *Chaos Ethics*. Parfit calls consequentialism an 'external rival' to morality in his epic two volume swansong, *On What Matters* (2011), and my views on Parfit are... well, you know the drill by now.

Consequentialist philosophers may feel that I am unfairly tarring them with the brush I am using to identify the gargantuan failures in this style of ethics. Indeed, they may well agree about the failures. I apologise to any consequentialist whose work pushes back against the problems I am outlining here – particularly Toby Ord – but the situation is now so completely and utterly out of hand that I think it might be time to throw consequentialism under the bus and produce entirely new forms of outcome-focused ethics, such as those proposed by Levi Bryant that will come up in the next chapter.

At the beginning of this section, I suggest some sadness at the popularity of 'Anthropocene' for describing our current time. The trouble with this term is that it is constructed to sound like a geological epoch – that's the precise reason this name is being suggested. But geological epochs last millennia. We will not last that long without making a radical change in our circumstances, something that I very much hope we are capable of making. If we do last that long, future geologists can certainly apply this term to our epoch. Right now, it is premature and utterly misleading to suggest what is happening in the wake of contemporary technological acceleration is the commencement of a new human-focussed geological epoch and not a boundary event – indeed, an extinction event that may yet claim our species as it has already claimed so many others. We still have time to solve our problems; there is still the possibility of an Anthropocene. But we still have much to do if we are to earn this.

Finally, my accusation that academia has paralysed itself by cloaking its conversations in anonymity is a reference to the core argument of *Wikipedia Knows Nothing*, that knowledge is a practice and that we are confused when we think the truth is going to emerge through enforcing double blind peer review – a ritualised masked conflict between academics that prevents those with common ground from forming an effective community. If peer review does not serve a community-building role (and currently it does the opposite, pitting learned folks against one another), academia is merely a convenient way of removing our intellectuals from the important conversations.

Chapter V
High Tech, Low Fidelity

In this chapter, I am channelling Ivan Illich. In particular, the critique of cars builds upon his astonishing *Energy and Equity* (1974) and the critique of medicine upon *Medical Nemesis* (1975). These books, along with *Tools for Conviviality* that I mentioned before, changed my life and remain as important to understanding our contemporary crisis as ever. Inspired by *Medical Nemesis*, I argue in *Chaos Ethics* for a 'duty to die' (Chapter 5, section 'The Duty to Die'), which is opposed to any and all kinds of techno-immortality.

Faith in What?

Unhusbands and unwives are discussed in *Chaos Ethics* (Chapter 5, section 'Unmarriage'), while the chimerical quality of 'faith versus reason' is a core theme in *The Mythology of Evolu-*

tion (2012).

Levi Bryant's novel conception of ethics in terms of the fragility of the future can be found in a paper he has written for the French journal *Multitude*. To my knowledge, this is not yet in print, but he shared a pre-print draft at his blog, *Larval Subjects*, entitled 'For an Ethics of the Fold' (2016). In an oh-so-object-oriented-ontology fashion, Levi talks about 'bodies' with complete ambiguity as to whether he is talking about microscopic creatures, cyborgs, cybergs, or anything else besides. What strikes me as valuable about his approach is that it is an outcome-focused ethics but its focus is the fragility of the future, and the way 'ought' concerns the relationship between present and future. I hope he and others will develop this thread further.

Aristotle's views on virtues and debilities appear in what is usually called the *Nicomachean Ethics*, although the translation I read went for the simpler title of *Ethics* (2009). It would be wrong for me to have got through an entire book discussing virtue and never mention Aristotle, who more-or-less founds the Western tradition of virtue ethics, but in the interests of avoiding our usual cultural myopia I led off with the Chinese virtue ethics traditions instead.

Alain Badiou is a philosopher for whom I have immeasurable respect, and who finally got me over my bugbear about Plato. The place to go for his moral philosophy is *Ethics: An Essay on the Understanding of Evil* (1998), the first work of his I read and the one I would still recommend as an entry point to his philosophy. My thinking doesn't align perfectly with Badiou, and I argue against him in *Chaos Ethics* on various points (e.g. Chapter 7, section 'Are Rights Wrong?'), but I have been greatly inspired by his way of thinking about truth as something that punctures the conventional order of existence in an inexplicable event. Yet I find it impossible to read Badiou's philosophy and not see religious themes, as his friend Slavoj Zizek has also accused.

As for Kierkegaard, once again it's the first book of his that I read that I would recommend as a starting place – *Fear and Trembling* (1843). The discussion of the 'leap of faith' in this work is astonishing, and slightly terrifying too. Did this book make me more willing to identify as a Christian (albeit, as one of five religions that I identify with...)? I am not sure of the chronology of events within my life, but certainly Kierkegaard is a Christian who I admire, and whom I wish more contemporary Christians would learn from. My discussion of Kierkegaard's existentialism is in *Chaos Ethics* Chapter 2, section 'Nietzsche's Abyss'.

The Dependent World

The influence of my black Labrador, Boomer, is undoubtedly felt here, as it has been elsewhere in my work. He appears, for instance, as a puppy in *Imaginary Games*, Chapter 1, section 'Biology of Play'. As mentioned in the main text, this book is also where you will find my discussion of Félix Ravaisson's notion of habit (Chapter 7, section 'Truth and Habit'). You can also go straight to the source, Ravaisson's *Of Habit* (1838), which Mark Vernon suggested to me when I was writing my first book of philosophy. Mark also has the dubious honour of being the first editor to reject my philosophical books, which in turn led to my work improving immensely.

The reference to *Wikipedia Knows Nothing* in the main text is largely self-contained, but I ought to take this opportunity once again to thank Chris Billows, since without his engagement with the original ideas on my blog that particular book would never have come about.

Ivan Illich's convivial tools were mentioned previously, with the relevant book being *Tools for Conviviality*. As I said at the beginning of this Author Notes section, this chapter has me channelling Illich, as the main text here now makes explicit. Also, and fulfilling my earlier remarked debt to Donna Haraway, here I draw attention to her later book, *The Companion Species Manifesto* (2003). This deserves as much or more attention than 'The Cyborg Manifesto', and the theme of dogs that frames this section directly aligns with Haraway's work.

My claim that the developed world has more to learn from the so-called Third World than vice versa is made in *Chaos Ethics* (Chapter 5, section 'Equality as Exclusion' and Chapter 9, section 'Beyond Cyberfetish'). It could be disputed – but thus far, I have only encountered knee-jerk reactions to this claim, and usually from people with absolutely no experience of the 'undeveloped' cultures they are judging. Finally, my use of the term 'heretic' here is inspired by Mark Vernon's final imprint for Acumen before they were swallowed up into the belly of the book-publishing cyberg.

Chapter VI
Technological Cowardice

The opening discussion of the concept of virtue in the heroic age comes (once again) from Alasdair MacIntyre's *After Virtue*, while the idea that we have lost sight of the inevitability of death is the core theme in Ivan Illich's *Medical Nemesis*.

The idea that Artificial Intelligence is limited by the absence of a world that the robot lives within was a key criticism advanced by Hubert Dreyfus in the 1970s, most famously in *What Computers Can't Do* (1972). The thesis that our understanding is intimately tied to being in a world can be related to the work of both Martin Heidegger and Maurice

Merleau-Ponty, with serious implications drawn out by Dreyfus and Charles Taylor in *Retrieving Realism* (2015). My discussions of their thesis form an important part of the arguments of *Wikipedia Knows Nothing*.

Regarding the role of the bully, it is difficult to suggest where to go for clarity. Psychologists are tying themselves up in knots about this and any source I could turn to will entail some serious limitations. For instance, I agree with Izzy Kalman (2013) that it is a mistake to try to use enforcement techniques to prevent bullying, and the methods he teaches to help people overcome bullying seem both reasonable and effective. But his suggestion that we should stop using the term 'bully' because it is a subjective insult and not an objective diagnosis both undervalues our human judgement and massively overvalues psychological research, which is never objective since it does not deal with objects but rather beings. Perhaps all I can do in a psychological context is agree with Julian Dooley and Donna Cross' conclusions in 'Cyberbullying Versus Face-to-Face Bullying: A Theoretical and Conceptual Review' (2009) that the psychological research is still getting up to speed in this area.

However, 'cowardice' is not a psychological description but a moral one – it is a negative judgement made against another's behaviour. While courage is a habit and thus a virtue, that of acting even when afraid, cowardice is not just the opposite of this. It *can* mean being overcome by fear, but it can also mean resorting to cowardly means. This is what I claim makes bullying an act of cowardice. Psychologically, we can often understand what the troll does as being motivated by moral horror, i.e. Leon Festinger's cognitive dissonance (1957): the bully, and especially the troll, dissipates their dissonance by making their victims *other*, and harassing them. Not coincidentally, this analysis also explains racism and other acts of cultural vengeance.

Bradley Strawser's original justifications for the use of armed drones can be found in 'Moral Predators: The Duty to Employ Uninhabited Aerial Vehicles' (2010), which eventually contributed to his book on the topic, although I have not read it. Additional commentary referred to in this part of the book mainly comes from an interview conducted by Rory Carroll (2012). Laurie Calhoun's outstanding report on the horrific practices of drone assassination can be found in her exemplary book *We Kill Because We Can: From Soldiering to Assassination in the Drone Age* (2015), and my own condemnation of this appalling insult to the bravery of soldiers can be found in *Chaos Ethics*, Chapter 7, section 'National Insecurity'. Ironically, military drone pilots may well show courage; their cowardice is primarily – like the internet troll – in their use of cowardly means, and this was ordered upon them.

Everybody's Got Justice Wrong Except You

On Nietzsche's analysis of the problems of morality, a good place to start would be the 1989 translation by Walter Kaufmann and R.J. Hollingdale of *On the Genealogy of Morals* (1887). My take on Nietzsche's position is in *Chaos Ethics*, Chapter 2, section 'Nietzsche's Abyss'. This also lays out my support of chaos in the context of ethics – although, as this book has aimed to clarify, fidelity remains essential to living a good life and to accept chaos ethics is in no way to give up on the idea of the good.

Moral representation is a concept that I expounded in the final chapter of *Chaos Ethics*, Chapter 9, section 'Moral Representation'. This concept was inspired by my engagement with Haidt, and is probably the greatest debt that I owe to him.

As for Wittgenstein's views of practices, and the role of a background of understanding, the original work from which this topic springboards is his incredible *Philosophical Investigations* (1962), which I can heartily recommend for anyone who feels like tackling some epic yet extremely worthwhile philosophy. However, in terms of understanding Wittgenstein's concept of a practice, my guide in recent years has been Peter Lamarque's outstanding essay 'Wittgenstein, Literature, and the Idea of a Practice' (2010). This is put to good use in *Chaos Ethics*, Chapter 4, section 'The Rules of Dogs', Chapter 5, section 'Fictional Values'.

Is The Truth Still Out There?

While there are hundreds of places I could send you for a discussion of the truth, the one that this chapter depends upon is the one I developed in *Wikipedia Knows Nothing*. It is here that I stake my claim for understanding knowledge as a practice, which initially seems strange (after all, doesn't knowing something literally mean being able to state the facts?) but the more I have worked with this idea, the clearer it seems that the encyclopaedia is a terribly poor substitute for actually knowing. Whether you know isn't just a matter of stating the facts, you have to actually possess the knowledge that goes with it. This is a point made brilliantly in Nicholas Roeg's film *Insignificance* (1985): Marilyn Monroe is able to recite the theory of relativity to Albert Einstein – but she has none of the knowledge required to understand what she is saying.

Although I was certainly affected by my encounter with Bruno Latour's work, it has been the influence of Isabelle Stengers upon him that has most influenced my own philosophy. I was completely transformed by the final part of

Cosmopolitics II (2003), 'The Curse of Tolerance', which was a huge influence on my *Chaos Ethics*. The concept of a 'reliable witness' as a way of understanding scientific experiments can be found in her *Power and Invention* (1997), although I confess to getting this idea into my head mostly through Latour's *Politics of Nature*.

Regarding Jacques Rancière's concept of dissensus, a great place to start is *Aesthetics and Its Discontents* (2004). There are many other books by Rancière that would also cover this idea, but this happens to be the one where I first encountered it, and it makes his case in a manner that is both accessible and persuasive.

Chapter VII
On more than one occasion I have been accused of bringing in new material into my conclusions. On this occasion, I hope to have curtailed this urge and merely tied together all the content that I have introduced earlier in the book.

References

Agence France-Presse (2014). 'Smartphone "zombies" wreak havoc on Japan's streets', *AFP*, available online: http://www.timeslive.co.za/scitech/2014/11/12/Smartphone-zombies-wreak-havoc-on-Japans-streets (accessed 31st March 2017).

Anderson, Benedict (1983). *Imagined Communities: Reflections on the Origin and Spread of Nationalism*, London: Verso.

Archetype Interactive (1995). *Meridian 59* [Online game], Redwood City, CA: The 3DO Company.

Aristotle (384-82 BC). *Ethics*, translated by D.P. Chase [2009], Boston, MA: MobileReference.

Atari (1985). *Gauntlet* [Arcade coin-op], Sunnyvale, CA: Atari, Inc.

Badiou, Alain (1998). *Ethics: An Essay on the Understanding of Evil*, translated by Peter Hallward [2001], New York, NY: Verso.

Bartle, Richard A. and Trubshaw, Roy (1978). *Essex MUD* or *MUD1* [Online game], no publisher.

Bartle, Richard A. (2015). *MMOs from the Outside In: The Massively Multiplayer Online Role-Playing Games of Psychology, Law, Government, and Real Life*, New York, NY: Apress.

Bateman, Chris (2011). *Imaginary Games*, Winchester and Chicago, IL: Zero Books.

Bateman, Chris (2014). *Chaos Ethics*, Winchester and Chicago, IL: Zero Books.

Bateman, Chris (2016a). *Wikipedia Knows Nothing*, Pittsburgh, PA: ETC Press.

Bateman, Chris (2016b). 'Playing Work or Gamification as Stultification', Presented at the *Work and Play* Conference 2016 (6th July), Salford.

Bateman, Chris (2016c). 'No-one Plays Alone', Presented at the First International Joint Conference of DiGRA and FDG 2016 (3rd August), Dundee.

Bateman, Chris (2017). 'Game Design Lineages: *Minecraft*'s Inventory', Presented at DiGRA UK 2017 (5th May), MediaCity, Salford.

Mark Blitz (2014). 'Understanding Heidegger on Technology', *The New Atlantis*, No. 41 (Winter), pp. 63-80.

Blizzard (2004). *World of Warcraft* [Online game], Irvine, CA: Blizzard Entertainment.

Bretzke, James T. (1995). 'The Tao of Confucian Virtue Ethics', *International Philosophical Quarterly*, vol. 35, no. 1, pp. 25-41.

Bryant, Levi (2016). 'For an Ethics of the Fold', available online: https://larvalsubjects.files.wordpress.com/2016/11/ethicalbodies.docx (accessed 26th March 2017).

Cadwalladr, Carole (2016). 'Google, democracy and the truth about internet search', *The Observer*, available online: https://www.theguardian.com/technology/2016/dec/04/google-democracy-truth-internet-search-facebook (accessed 24th March 2017).

Calhoun, Laurie (2015). *We Kill Because We Can: From Soldiering to Assassination in the Drone Age*, London: Zed Books.

Carroll, Rory (2012). 'The philosopher making the moral case for drones', *The Guardian*, available online: https://www.

theguardian.com/world/2012/aug/02/philosopher-moral-case-drones (accessed 26th March 2017).

Centers for Disease Control and Prevention (2016) 'Distracted Driving in the United Stats and Europe', cdc.gov, available online: https://www.cdc.gov/features/dsdistracteddriving/ accessed 22nd March 2017).

Cinematronics (1979). *Tail Gunner* [Arcade coin-op], El Cajon, CA: Cinematronics.

Clarke, Arthur C. (1962). 'Hazards of Prophecy: The Failure of Imagination' in *Profiles of the Future: An Enquiry into the Limits of the Possible*, London: The Scientific Book Club.

Delaune, Tom (2015). 'The Tao of Heidegger', presented at the *Western Political Science Association 2015 Annual Meeting*, Chinese Thought in Comparative Political Perspective Panel, Las Vegas, 3 April.

Deleuze, Gilles and Guattari, Félix (1991). *What Is Philosophy?*, translated by Hugh Tomlinson and Graham Burchell [1996], New York and Chichester: Columbia University Press.

Dooley, Julian and Cross, Donna (2009). 'Cyberbullying Versus Face-to-Face Bullying: A Theoretical and Conceptual Review', *Journal of Psychology*, vol. 217, pp. 182-188.

Dreyfus, Hubert (1972), *What Computers Can't Do*, New York, NY: MIT Press.

Dreyfus, Hubert and Taylor, Charles (2015). *Retrieving Realism*, Cambridge, MA: Harvard University Press.

Duggan, Maeve (2014). 'Online Harassment', *Pew Research Center*, available online: http://www.pewinternet.org/2014/10/22/online-harassment/ (accessed 30th March

2017).

Farmer, Randy and Glass, Bryce (2010). *Building Web Reputation Systems*, Sebastopol, CA: O'Reilly Media.

Ferster, Charles and Skinner, B. F. (1957). *Schedules of reinforcement*, New York, NY: Appleton-Century-Crofts.

Festinger, Leon (1957). *A Theory of Cognitive Dissonance*, Stanford, CA: Stanford University Press.

Gray, J.W. (2011). 'Review of The Emotional Dog and its Rational Tail', *Ethical Realism*, available online: https://ethical-realism.wordpress.com/2011/11/02/review-of-the-emotional-dog-and-its-rational-tail/ (accessed 25th March 2017).

Green, Brian (2017). 'Series on online anonymity and privacy, parts 1-4', *Psychochild's Blog*, available online: http://psychochild.org/?p=1465, http://psychochild.org/?p=1466, http://psychochild.org/?p=1467, http://psychochild.org/?p=1468 (accessed 24th March 2017).

Gualeni, Stefano (2015). *Virtual Worlds as Philosophical Tools: How to Philosophize with a Digital Hammer*, New York, NY: Palgrave Macmillan.

Gygax, Gary and Arneson, Dave (1974). *Dungeons & Dragons* [Tabletop game], Lake Geneva, WA, Tactical Studies Rules, Inc.

Haidt, Jonathan (2001). 'The Emotional Dog and its Rational Tail: A Social Intuitionist Approach to Moral Judgment', *Psychological Review*, no. 108, pp. 814-834.

Haraway, Donna (1991). 'Cyborg Manifesto: Science, Technology, and Socialist-Feminism in the Late Twentieth Century' in *Simians, Cyborgs and Women: The Reinvention of Nature*, New York, NY: Routledge, pp. 149-192.

Haraway, Donna (2003). *The Companion Species Manifesto: Dogs, People, and Significant Otherness*, Chicago, IL: Prickly Paradigm Press.

Harman, Graham (1999). *Tool-being: Elements in a theory of objects*. Ph.D. thesis, DePaul University.

Heidegger, Martin (1954) *The Question Concerning Technology, and Other Essays*, translated by William Lovitt [1977]. New York: Harper and Row.

Illich, Ivan (1973). *Tools for Conviviality,* London and New York: Marion Boyars.

Illich, Ivan (1974). *Energy and Equity*, London: Harper and Row.

Illich, Ivan (1975). *Medical Nemesis: The Expropriation of Health*, London: Marion Boyers.

Insignificance (1985) [Movie], London: Palace Pictures.

Introna, Lucas D. (2009). 'Ethics and the speaking of things', *Theory, Culture and Society*, vol. 26, no. 4, pp. 398-419.

Kalman, Israel C. (2013). 'Why Psychology is Failing To Solve the Problem of Bullying', *International Journal on World Peace*, vol. 30, no. 2, pp. 71-97.

Kant, Immanuel (1785). *Groundwork for the Metaphysics of Morals*, edited and translated by Allen W. Wood [2002], New Haven, CT: Yale University Press.

Kearl, Holly (2014). 'Unsafe and Harassed in Public Spaces', *Stop Street Harassment*, available online: http://www.stopstreetharassment.org/wp-content/uploads/2012/08/2014-National-SSH-Street-Harassment-Report.pdf (accessed 30th March 2017).

Key, Ed and David Kanaga (2012). *Proteus* [PC Game], privately published.

Kierkegaard, Søren (1843). *Fear and Trembling: A Dialectical Lyric by Johannes de Silentio*, translated by Alastair Hannay [2006], London: Penguin.

Korsgaard, Christine (1997). 'The Normativity of Instrumental Reason' in Garrett Cullity and Berys Gaut (eds.), *Ethics and Practical Reason*, Oxford: Oxford University Press, pp. 213-54.

Koster, Raph. (2005). *A Theory of Fun for Game Design*, Scottsdale, AZ: Paraglyph Press.

Lamarque, Peter (2010). 'Wittgenstein, Literature, and the Idea of a Practice', *British Journal of Aesthetics* vol. 50, no. 4, pp. 375-388.

Latour, Bruno (1994). 'On Technical Mediation', *Common Knowledge*, vol. 3, no. 2, pp. 29–64.

Latour, Bruno (2002). 'Morality and Technology: The End of the Means', translated by Couze Venn, *Theory, Culture & Society*, vol. 19, no. 5/6, pp. 247-260.

Latour, Bruno (1999). *Politics of Nature: How to Bring the Sciences into Democracy*, translated by Catherine Porter [2004], Cambridge, MA: Harvard University Press.

Latour, Bruno (2005). *Reassembling the Social: An Introduction to Actor-Network-Theory*, Oxford: Oxford University Press.

MacIntyre, Alasdair (1984). *After Virtue: A Study in Moral Theory*, second edition, Notre Dame, IN: University of Notre Dame Press.

MacIntyre, Alasdair (1990). *Three Rival Versions of Moral Enquiry: Encyclopaedia, Genealogy, and Tradition*, London: Gerald Duckworth & Company. Ltd.

Maxis (2002). *The Sims Online* [Online game], Redwood City, CA: Electronic Arts.

Mazzocchi, Phyllis (2015). 'Play as a Portal to Awakening in the Blithesome Wanderings of Chuang Tzu', presented at *Philosophy at Play* (9th June), Gloucester.

McGonigal, Jane (2011). *Reality is Broken: Why Games Make Us Better and How They Can Change the World*, London: J. Cape.

Midgley, Mary (1985). *Evolution as a Religion: Strange hopes and stranger fears*, London and New York, NY: Methuen.

Midgley, Mary (1992). *Science as Salvation: A Modern Myth and its Meaning*, London and New York, NY: Routledge.

Mighty (2016). 'Palm Oil's Black Box', available online: http://www.mightyearth.org/wp-content/uploads/2016/07/Olam-technical-report_Dec-9_with-images_lowres1-002.pdf (accessed 12th May 2017).

Mill, John Stuart (1859). *On Liberty*, London: John W. Parker and Son.

Moyal, Ann (1989). 'The Feminine Culture of the Telephone: People, Patterns and Policy', *Prometheus*, vol. 7 no. 1, pp. 5–31.

Newtoy (2009). *Words with Friends* [Online game], McKinney, TX: Newtoy.

Niantic (2016). *Pokémon Go* [Augmented reality game], San Francisco, CA: Niantic.

Nietzsche, Friedrich (1887). *On the Genealogy of Morals*, translated by Walter Kaufmann and R.J. Hollingdale [1989], New

York, NY: Vintage Books.

Noble, Grant (1987). 'Discriminating Between the Intrinsic and Instrumental Telephone User', *Australian Journal of Communication*, no. 11, pp. 63–85.

Obeidallah, Dean (2012). 'A day without a cell phone', *CNN*, available online: http://www.cnn.com/2012/09/26/opinion/ obeidallah-cell-phone/index.html (accessed 31st March 2017).

Parfit, Derek (2011). *On What Matters*, Volume 1 and 2, Oxford: Oxford University Press.

Persson, Marcus and Bergensten, Jens (2009). *Minecraft* [Videogame]. Stockholm: Mojang.

Rancière, Jacques (1987). *The Ignorant Schoolmaster: Five Lessons in Intellectual Emancipation*, translated by Kristen Ross [1991], Stanford, CA: Stanford University Press.

Rancière, Jacques (2004). *Aesthetics and Its Discontents*, translated by Steven Corcoran [2009], Cambridge: Polity Press.

Ravaisson, Félix (1838). *Of Habit*, translated by Clare Carlisle [2008], London: Continuum.

Riot Games (2009). *League of Legends* [Online game], Los Angeles, CA: Riot Games.

Saidi, Nicole (2012). 'Readers: Are we headed for a smartphone zombie apocalypse?', *CNN*, available online: http:// www.cnn.com/2012/10/03/tech/smartphone-zombie-apocalypse-comments/ (accessed 31st March 2017).

Sharp, Mark (2015). 'Beware the smartphone zombies blindly wandering around Hong Kong', *South China Morning Post*, available online: http://www.scmp.com/lifestyle/technology/article/1725001/smartphone-zombies-are-putting-your-life-and-theirs-danger?page=all (accessed 31st March 2017).

Star Trek (1966-1969) [Television show], Los Angeles, CA: De-silu Productions

Stengers, Isabelle (1997). *Power and Invention: Situating Science*, Minneapolis: University of Minnesota Press.

Stengers, Isabelle (2003). *Cosmopolitics II*, translated by Robert Bononno [2011], Minneapolis, MN: University of Minnesota Press.

Stengers, Isabelle (2012). 'Reclaiming Animism', *e-Flux*, vol. 36, available online: http://www.e-flux.com/journal/re-claiming-animism/ (accessed: 22 March 2017).

Strawser, Bradley J. (2010). 'Moral Predators: The Duty to Employ Uninhabited Aerial Vehicles', *Journal of Military Ethics*, vol. 9, no. 4, pp. 343-368.

Taylor, Charles (2007). *A Secular Age*, Cambridge, MA: Belknap of Harvard.

Teschner, George and Tomasi, Alessandro (2009). 'Technological Paradigm in Ancient Taoism', *Techné: Research in Philosophy and Technology*, vol. 13, no. 3, available online: https://scholar.lib.vt.edu/ejournals/SPT/v13n3/teschner.html (accessed 8th May 2017).

The Terminator (1984) [Movie], Los Angeles, CA: Orion Pictures Corporation.

Terminator: Salvation (2009) [Movie], Culver City, CA: Columbia Pictures Industries.

Turkle, Sherry (2011). *Alone Together: Why We Expect More From Technology and Less From Each Other*, New York, NY: Basic Books.

US Department of Transportation (2016). 'What is distracted driving?', *Distraction.gov*, available online: https://www.distraction.gov/stats-research-laws/facts-and-statistics.html (accessed 22nd March 2017).

Verbeek, Peter-Paul (2006). 'Materializing Morality: Design Ethics and Technological Mediation', *Science, Technology, & Human Values*, vol. 31, no. 3 (May), pp. 361-380.

Waley, Arthur (1958). *The Way and Its Power: Lao Tzu's Tao Te Ching and Its Place in Chinese Thought*, New York, NY: Grove Press.

Watson, Burton (1968). *The Complete Works of Chuang Tzu*, New York, NY: Columbia University Press.

Whitehead, Alfred North (1929). *Process and Reality*, New York: Macmillan.

Wittgenstein, Ludwig (1962). *Philosophical Investigations*, translated by G.E.M. Anscombe, New York, NY: Macmillan.

Wood, Allen W. (1999). *Kant's Ethical Thought*, Cambridge: Cambridge University Press.

Wood, Allen (2008). *Kantian Ethics*, New York, NY: Cambridge University Press.

Zhao, Yanxia (2015). 'The Spirit of Charity and Compassion in Daoist Religion', *Sociology and Anthropology*, vol. 3, no. 2, pp. 122-135.

Acknowledgements

My academic debts are outlined above, but my personal debts warrant their own remarks. First and foremost, to Todd Swift for offering me a book with his small press on the strength of *Imaginary Games*, without any clue as to what I was going to deliver! I count myself inordinately lucky to have landed such a wonderful editor with so little effort on my part. I must also thank Rosanna Hildyard, whose final copyedits showed such meticulous care and respect of the nuances of the text that it bordered upon the miraculous.

I extend grateful thanks to all the players of the 'Cybervirtue Campaign' on my blog, *Only a Game*, who participated in discussions around the topics that have coalesced into this book, and also to those on the edge, participating via Twitter or Google+. This includes, at the very least, Richard Bartle, Edmund Berger, Chris Billows, Ari Cheslow, Peter Crowther, Dirk Felleman, Joel Goodwin, Brian Green, Tom H., Malte Kosian, Justin Robertson, Víctor Navarro Remesal, Rik Newman, and Bart Stewart. Of these, I also extend special gratitude to Víctor Navarro Remesal – the first writer anywhere in the world to buy into my concept of 'cybervirtue' and write on this topic, and to Brian Green for his extended discussion on privacy and anonymity, as well as for his support in what I have been trying to explore here.

I must give especial thanks to Babette Babich for our stimulating public dialogues that touched upon many of the topics of this book, and part of which ran in parallel to the Cybervirtue Campaign, helping bring yet more people to the table. I owe a substantial debt to the pre-readers of this manuscript Pat Bennett, Peter Berger, Ari Cheslow, and Chris Billows, who provided diverse and illuminating feedback that proved utterly invaluable, and to others who helped provide perspective on the draft such as Dan Cook, who kept me honest in representing free-to-play, and Maggie Greene for advice on transliterations of Chinese names. In this as in all things, I am better for the love and support of others.

Finally, in this as with all my books, my thanks to my wife Adria, my boys, Soren, Leto, and Blake, and my dog Boomer. You not only gave me the space to write this manuscript, but the reason to persevere with it. My wife's question: 'Are you playing on your "crackphone" again?' — an accusation that I was ultimately able to level against her as well! — formed an important background to the long and ponderous thoughts that led inexorably to this book.

May we all endeavour to be virtuous cyborgs together.

You do everything on your smartphone and love it – you are, now and forevermore, a cyborg. But how would you know if you were a *good* cyborg?

Game designer and philosopher Chris Bateman explores cyborg virtue through problems such as cyberbullying, 'fake news', and the indifference of computers to human needs. Bateman reveals our shallow-sightedness in the face of the unfathomable complexity of our cybernetic networks. Critical yet optimistic, *The Virtuous Cyborg* rises to the challenge of the twenty-first century by asking us to ponder the question of what kind of cyborgs we want to become.

Dr Chris Bateman is an outsider philosopher, game designer, and author. Graduating with a Masters degree in Artificial Intelligence/Cognitive Science, he has since pursued highly-acclaimed independent research into how and why people play games, and was the first person in the world to gain a Doctorate in the aesthetics of play experiences. He works in the digital entertainment industry as an expert in game design and narrative, and has nearly fifty published game credits, including the acclaimed *Discworld Noir* and *Ghost Master*.

'The future is coming at us fast, and Chris Bateman is a masterful guide to the most urgent questions we face there.'
– Jane McGonigal
'...highlights our often myopic view of the cyber networks we find ourselves living in, teasing out the underlying ethical issues with compelling clarity.'
– Justin Robertson
'Bateman's proposal of cybervirtue might be a clever way of sneaking a new gentler human spirit into society at large.'
– Michaël Samyn

'Bateman brings a fresh and vigorous philosophical voice to explore virtue theory and cyborgs, robots, and AI, including classical and cutting edge ethical debates.'
— Babette Babich